PRAISE FOR AK TURNER

"At last . . . a kindred spirit. AK Turner finds the funny—strike that—the hilarity in life's everyday circumstances. Her candid yet heartwarming look at parenting is a master class in authenticity and just plain fun."
—**Joely Fisher, actress, singer, and author of** *Growing Up Fisher*

"Brutal honesty and boozy hilarity.
Turner deserves to have a cocktail named after her."
—**Jen Mann,** *New York Times* **bestselling**
author of *People I Want to Punch in the Throat*

"This sincere, laugh-out-loud confessional from Turner candidly reveals and revels in the flaws and dysfunctions of the author and her family. Turner is not afraid to voice her private thoughts and never takes herself too seriously. She details her pregnancy and child-rearing techniques in a refreshingly honest way. The book is lighthearted and riddled with comedic episodes that young mothers in particular will relate to and enjoy."
—*Publishers Weekly*

"Did Erma Bombeck ever guzzle vodka? If she did, she might have come close to the ribald domestic humor in Turner's 'memoir' *This Little Piggy Went to the Liquor Store*."
—*The Quivering Pen*

"AK Turner's witty essays explore the raw realities of raising children so they won't become serial killers, how to deal with dinner guests who proudly arrive with tater tot casserole, and how to survive when you accidentally poop your pants more than your kid does."
—**Elaine Ambrose,** *Midlife Happy Hour*

"Empty bladder before reading."
—**Laurie Notaro,** *New York Times* **bestselling author of**
The Idiot Girls' Action-Adventure Club

"It's rare for a writer to actually make me laugh out loud, but AK Turner does just that."
—Robin O'Bryant, *New York Times* bestselling author of *Ketchup Is a Vegetable and Other Lies Moms Tell Themselves*

"I laughed out loud . . . but make no mistake, this book is equally heartfelt and humorous as AK Turner delves into all the wonders, challenges, and horrifying playground moments of parenting— the most extreme sport there is."
—Cameron Morfit, *Sports Illustrated*

"Reading AK Turner's *This Little Piggy Went to the Liquor Store* is like going to your neighbor's house for a play date and discovering that she's just as clueless and crazy as you are."
—Stacy Dymalski, *Confessions of a Band Geek Mom*

"AK Turner is the best friend that we dream of having: someone who is smart and eloquent and doesn't take herself or her life too seriously. That is what makes all of her books so fabulous, you can't help but envision yourself right alongside of her, cheering her on, laughing out loud, and thanking your lucky stars that you have her in your life."
—Lynn Morrison, *The Nomad Mom Diary*

"AK Turner can turn even the simplest family story into a rollicking, outrageous, hilarious adventure. Buckle up!"
—Michelle Newman, *You're My Favorite Today*

"Absolutely hilarious . . . absolutely amazing."
—*Book Loving Hippo*

This Little Piggy
Went to the Liquor Store

This Little Piggy
Went to the Liquor Store

UNAPOLOGETIC ADMISSIONS FROM A NON-CONTENDER
FOR MOTHER OF THE YEAR

AK Turner

BROWN BOOKS
PUBLISHING GROUP

This Little Piggy Went to the Liquor Store
Unapologetic Admissions From a Non-Contender for Mother of the Year

Brown Books Publishing Group
16250 Knoll Trail Drive, Suite 205
Dallas, Texas 75248
www.BrownBooks.com
(972) 381-0009

A New Era in Publishing®

Names: Turner, A. K. (Amanda K.)
Title: This little piggy went to the liquor store : unapologetic admissions
    from a non-contender for Mother of the Year / AK Turner.
Description: Dallas, Texas : Brown Books Publishing Group, [2018] |
    Originally published: [Boise, Idaho] : Fever Streak Press, 2012.
Identifiers: ISBN 9781612542775
Subjects: LCSH: Turner, A. K. (Amanda K.)--Family--Humor. |
    Motherhood--Humor. | Mother and child--Travel--Humor. | LCGFT:
    Humor.
Classification: LCC PS3620.U758 Z46 2018 | DDC 817/.6092--dc23

ISBN 978-1-61254-277-5
LCCN 2018937721

Printed in the United States
10 9 8 7 6 5 4 3 2 1

Design by Sarah Tregay, Designworks, Inc.
Author photo by LeAna Earley

For more information or to contact the author, please go to
www.AKTurner.com

For Mike.

And not just because he's really good-looking.

But mostly.

CONTENTS

INTRODUCTION

If you'd told twenty-year-old me that someday I'd have a husband, two kids, a home in Idaho, and spend a few months of every year traveling the world, I'd have called you crazy. Looney, high, and out of your gourd. Maybe I'd accept the traveling-the-world bit. That part is kick-ass. But married with kids in Idaho? Forget it. Ew. No thanks. I was allergic to even the thought of domesticity. Phrases like "parent-teacher association" and "Mommy and Me class" and "easy, lowfat, one-skillet weeknight dinners" made me break out in hives. I would live a life free of diaper bags and Crock-Pots and the burden of having to remember a wedding anniversary.

I was sure of it.

This is why twenty-year-olds are so adorably ignorant. I was as sure of my solitary path as I was when I asserted that we would never look back on eighties fashion and laugh, like we did with the styles of the sixties and seventies, because eighties fashion was totally normal. Nothing to make fun of there. Scrunchies, jelly shoes, bangles, side ponies, leg warmers, and jeans rolled up in a tight little above-the-ankle cuff were timeless, right? Just like Audrey Hepburn?

This book offers a small sampling of the idiotic times in my life. The embarrassing moments of childhood and agonizing blunders of adulthood, all here for your reading pleasure. Through all those misadventures, and sometimes because of them, I ended up with the life I'd never expected. Finding what you didn't know you wanted brings with it a varied cast of characters, from colorful relatives and childhood friends to asshole salesmen, drunken cops, and that lady in the grocery store who thinks it's acceptable to rub a pregnant stranger's belly. They're all part of the story that I never saw coming.

The traveling-the-world part? Yes, it's as kick-ass as I'd hoped. But equally awesome are my daughters, especially now that they let me sleep through the night and we're finally beyond diaper bags. My husband could not possibly be a better partner (or hotter), and doesn't seem to mind when I announce that my intentions for dinner have fallen through and we'll instead be dining on beer and peanuts.

And my wedding anniversary is August 5th.

I'm sure of it.

* * *

CHAPTER 1

Please Pass the Solitude

Growing up, my family resembled *The Brady Bunch*, mixed with suppressed anger, mental instability, and large quantities of alcohol. We had the usual amount of familial dysfunction—my parents divorced at the same time that a couple down the street divorced. Spouses swapped and remarried. I hate the word "swapping"; it makes the entire situation sound much more sordid than it probably was. Sordid or not, the end result left me with step-siblings twice over, as my mother married their father, which was a limited engagement, and my father married their mother, which continues to this day. It helps to have a flow chart to keep it all straight.

My best friend, Nora, lived in the costume room of a theater where her mother worked as the hair stylist. Mornings greeted her with looming, wigged mannequins and the mustiness of costumes that survived too many productions in a theater that couldn't afford dry cleaning. It was that or be homeless. Although, I think living in a theater's costume room because you have nowhere else to go technically *does* make you homeless. Beyond homelessness, Nora was very nearly named Hatshepsut and didn't meet her sperm-donor father until her teens.

Nora and I were two parts of a trio of high school friends. Ingrid completed the triangle as a straight-A student and ballet dancer with a golden voice, enviable intelligence, and long, expensive-looking, blonde hair. Nora and I pined dreamily for Ingrid's storybook life. She had a little sister, a mother, a father, and a dog, and they all lived happily together in the same house. Not an apartment or basement or townhouse, but a real house with a yard and shutters and a porch with hanging plants, and seasonal decorations that were culturally neutral, not too cutesy, and never left out too long. Her mother baked cookies, then *decorated* them, and never, ever let her hair down. It resided in a perpetual French twist.

You'd think that Nora and I would have milked our time in Ingrid's home, soaking in the perks of wealth. There was a guest bathroom, and not only was there liquid hand soap, but lotion as well. The luxurious and flaw-free couches had obviously not been acquired at a garage sale, or worse, found lingering and lonesome on a curb with a sign reading "FREE!" in Magic Marker. But we were never comfortable enough to enjoy the surroundings. We couldn't smoke or incorporate the word "fuck" three times into each sentence. Being there made us feel poor.

Then one day Ingrid's mother found a trash bag full of pot in their basement and confronted Ingrid's father, who announced that he was moving into an apartment downtown with his much younger girlfriend. The white picket fence splintered, and the picture window shattered. Ingrid chopped off her long, blonde locks, dyed her hair black, and went Goth.

Our envy of Ingrid's life dissipated, except for coveting the fact that she now had high drama juicier than anything lamentable in our own lives. Recognition for personal achievements was good, but even better was being acclaimed for something really horrible. Sometimes I daydreamed of acquiring sudden and inexplicable genius, but more often I longed to wake with a rare and debilitating disease, of which one of the side effects would be unparalleled beauty.

Watching Ingrid's family crumble, and considering the twisted family trees from which Nora and I grew, made me realize what a farce the storybook family was. As a result, by my late teens I decided that I never wanted a family of my own. In fact, I didn't even want the one I had. Through my parents' multiple marriages, I'd acquired myriad step-siblings, grandparents, cousins, aunts, and uncles, far more relatives than anyone could actually need or want. I'm a minimalist when it comes to things like family. A small family means lighter baggage to deal with, fewer gifts to buy and funerals to attend, infrequent interventions to stave off, and a smaller number of people who will read this and be offended.

I decided to forgo the troubles of both marriage and children. The inkling that family life was not for me came well before the teenage years. By the age of six, I knew that while my mother loved her daughters, parenthood exhausted her.

"I'll just rest my eyes, just for a minute," she'd say at the end of the day.

I'd perch bedside.

"Mom, are you awake?"

"No."

"Are you still sleeping?"

"Yes."

"What's for dinner? Can I have a filing cabinet?" Because what six-year-old doesn't want a filing cabinet? Also on my wish list were: desk, globe, and briefcase.

When I grew to realize that a world existed outside of my own, it further occurred to me that my sister and I might be what my mother often referred to as "a royal pain in the ass."

"Mom, am I a royal pain in your ass?" I asked.

"What do you mean? Of course not! Where did you hear that?"

"You say it all the time."

"Oh. Well, that's hardly relevant. Why would you ask such a thing?"

"Well, just think of all the things you could do if you didn't have to take care of Jennie and I."

"Jennie and *me*," she corrected. The conversation deteriorated into a lesson on grammar but left a hovering hint of truth.

The teen years solidified my cynicism. Thoughts of marriage and children prompted an immediate and negative response, because they necessitated vulnerability and tenderness. I was going for something more like coldhearted bitch. It seemed a good fit, like someone who has natural mathematic skills pursuing a career in finance.

My friends didn't share my lack of emotional aspirations, so I can't blame my condition on them. As my twenties loomed, I found myself convinced that anyone who entered into a potentially lifelong romantic relationship had made a terrible mistake and evidenced horrific judgment, akin to jumping onto subway tracks to retrieve a fallen pen. I mean, who would do such a thing? Pens are all the same and you can get them free at the bank and the Jiffy Lube. And if you jump onto the tracks, the train will likely come before you can scramble out, killing you in a manner both grotesque and meaningless. I had other plans.

Then, at the age of twenty-one, I met Mike. Nature began taking all of my assertions and flushing them carelessly down the commode of wayward plans. Hormones turned the ice crystals of my heart into warm oatmeal. I gleefully jumped onto the subway tracks, because I wanted *that* pen. The attraction was immediate, undeniable, and thankfully reciprocal.

Luckily, my future husband agreed to skip children. If we reproduced, our kids would inherit crooked teeth, poor vision, acne, psoriasis, and uncontrollable flatulence, all contained within a body not likely to grow much beyond five feet tall. That was just the outward, physical legacy. They'd also have to contend with obsessive-compulsive tendencies, a love of vice, and rampant bitchiness. I don't feel a need to identify which traits would come from which parent; suffice it to say, we felt it our duty not to pass these afflictions on to another human.

After agreeing that we wouldn't have kids, my thoughts turned directly to my in-laws. This would make me a disappointment, a cold fish, the selfish daughter-in-law. My failure to produce grandchildren would undeniably confirm to the family that I was an emotionally stunted and heartless abnormality. I was okay with that.

* * *

CHAPTER 2

Turner-Speak

When it came to our hypothetical children, and they had to be hypothetical because we weren't going to *have* children (I was sure of this—I was also young and naïve), I considered what traits could be blamed on our greater respective gene pools. My side of the family would have to take credit for a number of insecurities, addictions, and character defects. Which flaws would be attributable to the strange creatures people referred to as "Turners," whom I now called my in-laws?

Before I dish on them, I have to say that while Mike's family has dysfunctional aspects, as any family does, they also have qualities that warm my frigid little heart. I'm appreciative of their tolerance, as my neurotic tendencies are completely at odds with their sense of reason. They accept me for the controlling, compulsively cleaning, wine-guzzling Queen Bitch that I truly am.

Still, they have their quirks, and when they engage in Turner-Speak, I actively fight to keep that bitch from laughing out loud.

Turner-Speak is a linguist's nightmare. I've always been a word snob, yet I married into a family that is rife with malapropism and creates their own language as they need it. Words and phrases constantly merge, evolve, and adopt new meanings.

While explaining the vagaries of real estate, Mike used the phrase "fast or femine." I was wondering what exactly a "femine" was when I realized he meant "feast or famine."

My in-laws also fall prey to word spells when they're caught openmouthed and entranced by words they encounter in the world. My mother-in-law and I were browsing through Costco when she stopped abruptly in the middle of the sea of inching carts; a display had her curiously paralyzed.

"Memory Foam," she announced, nodding solemnly. "Memory Foam." She then returned to consciousness and proceeded without another word. Instances like this are pretty "run of the muck" (run of the mill + run amok), which, as far as I can tell, means either "commonplace" or "to attack furiously."

They make use of many common hybrids, like "supposably," but much of their vocabulary is more creative. A sampling of popular Turnerisms:

* * *

Dwelve

Practical usage: That's something we can dwelve into more another time.

How they came up with it: dwell + delve.

* * *

Substanance

Practical usage: A salad won't do; I need some real substanance.

How they came up with it: substance + sustenance.

* * *

Balslamic
What they really mean: balsamic.
How they came up with it: balsamic + Islamic?

* * *

Marianade
What they really mean: the verb "marinate" or the noun "mari-
nade."
Practical usage: Pass me the balslamic so I can make a marianade in which I'll marianade the beef.

* * *

Snidbits
What they really mean: small pieces of information.
How they came up with it: snippets + tidbits.

* * *

The first time I heard my husband say, "Nip it in the butt," I
laughed.

"I think you mean 'nip it in the *bud.*'"

"What?! That doesn't make any sense. It's 'nip it in the *butt.*'"

"No, *bud.* As in, cut off the bud of a plant before it grows.
Stop a problem before it starts."

"That's ridiculous," he said.

"Oh really? Then explain to me 'nip it in the butt.'"

"You know, like a little nip on the butt." With that, he used a
hand to mimic the opening and closing of a jaw, as if the phrase
originated from a pack of hostile dogs that threatened to nip at

unsuspecting buttocks.

All members of my husband's immediate family are proficient in malapropism. "You're a wordy person," Mike's sister Sandi said. "Where does the phrase 'like white on rye' come from?"

"You mean, 'like white on *rice*'?" I asked.

"Oh." She looked sullen. "I guess that makes more sense."

My mother-in-law is by far the most capable member of the family when it comes to mispronunciation. One of the first towns in which Mike and I lived together was Benicia, California. The conversation with her was as follows:

"We're moving to a town called Benicia."

"Valencia?"

"No, it's called Benicia."

"Benincia?"

"Benicia."

"Venetian?"

"No, Benicia."

"Benicia?"

"Yes! That's it, Benicia!"

"Okay, got it. Veninicia. I'm writing it down so I won't forget."

* * *

My brother-in-law was born Robert but legally changed his name to Virgil over a decade ago. Members of his family had a hard time taking him seriously when he did this, and some were a tad pissed off about it, but with time comes a certain measure of (if not total) acceptance.

"Shaka-khan, your mom!" This is Virgil's all-purpose greeting and means of announcing his presence. I'm not sure where it came from, but my guess is it's his way of expressing how cool he believes himself to be, while simultaneously dissing your mother.

After we relocated from Benicia to Boise, Idaho, Virgil came to visit us and assist in a few construction projects. (Our new home was barely habitable.) One evening after a difficult day's work, while sitting around a bonfire in our backyard, drinking beer and smoking cigarettes, Virgil began doing what he does best, telling stories.

"And so there I am and I'm drunk and I'm in this jail cell and no one will come and get me so I have to spend the night there. And it's so fucking cold and I'm so fucking scared that this four-hundred-pound Samoan dude is going to try to touch my butthole. And I'm on this steel cot and I swear my fucking balls are freezing, like really freezing, and I'm afraid they're going to be permanently damaged, so I'm cradling them with my hands, because, at this point, I'm thinking this is going to kill all my sperm and I'll never be able to have kids. So I'm cradling my balls, massaging my balls, but I'm afraid this Samoan dude is going to think that's an invitation, like I'm asking him to come fuck me in the ass, which is scaring the shit out of me. And then I think, well, maybe if I *take* a shit in the honey bucket, this guy won't want to come near my butthole."

As he spoke, the volume and profanity increased. We knew that our Mormon neighbors, who earlier that day brought us a snack of graham crackers pasted with frosting and sprinkles, couldn't help but hear. But you can't shut Virgil up. So you laugh now and apologize later.

"Virgil, keep it down a bit," I chided. "You're going to get us in trouble with the neighbors."

"Oh, sorry," he said, his voice dropping to a whisper. He

looked sheepish for a moment, but Virgil wanted an audience. Pissing off the neighbors would be a bonus. He proved this with his change in topic.

"Porn is great, but I fucking *love* granny porn. Seriously, I know it's fucked up, but that shit gets me off. Granny porn is the *best*."

"Granny porn?" I asked, taking the bait.

"Oh yeah." He nodded, as if speaking of the grail itself.

"You're making this up," I countered.

"Nooooo! Granny porn *rocks*!" He outlined the wonders of granny porn for us, and I realized that I should have just let him continue on about his freezing balls and the obese Samoan cellmate.

The only time I've ever seen Virgil at a loss for words is when confronted with a strikingly beautiful woman, at which time I think he finally shuts up because he's concentrating so desperately hard on not jizzing in his pants.

We often hire Virgil for odd jobs. He'll do anything, from installing an electrical outlet to scooping poop. I took him with me to clean out an abandoned home. The deadbeat tenants left a full fridge and an unpaid power bill, a notoriously deadly combination. I warned Virgil about it ahead of time.

"You're going to clean out the fridge, and it's going to be pretty rank."

"No problem," he assured me. "However nasty it is, I guarantee you I've encountered nastier things in my life." He was silent for a moment, searching for a story, not wanting to waste a good segue. "I dated this girl once with three nipples, which was totally hot, but she also had this fungus—"

His phone rang, cutting him off and robbing me of the

answers to many remaining questions. Does a third nipple imply a third breast? How did he know it wasn't simply an unfortunate birthmark? Was the fungus related to the nipple? Paramount to all of that, why on earth did they break up? But Virgil had been awaiting this phone call and immediately answered. One of his side jobs was hot-tub cleaning, and he'd contacted a specialist regarding matters beyond his expertise.

"Yeah, thanks for calling me back. I just wondered if you could tell me what it means when I fill the tub and then there's this foam and it's like, yelly brish?"

Virgil sometimes gets flustered when speaking on the phone, and the genetic deficiencies of language that all Turners share come to a head. By "yelly brish," he meant "yellowish brown." I'd been a Turner long enough to speak the language, but wondered if the person on the other end of the phone could decode him.

"And there's this film oily," he continued.

After a brief exchange, he hung up the phone and took note of my smirk.

"What?" he asked.

"So, you've got a yelly brish film oily?" I asked.

"What are you *talking* about? That doesn't even make any *sense*."

"But that's what you said on the phone," I explained.

"*What* was what I said on the phone?" he demanded.

"You said 'yelly brish' and 'film oily.'"

"Oh, *right*." Pause. "I did *not* say that." Pause. "Did I say that? Really? You're just fucking with me, right? Or does that lady seriously think I'm a moron now?"

"I don't know what she thinks, Virgil."

"Why'd you tell me? I hate you. I'm just kidding."

"You'll definitely hate me after you see this fridge," I said. "We're here."

"Bring it."

We didn't speak for the next fifteen minutes, spent unloading cleaning supplies and setting up.

"Holy Mother of GOD!" he announced when opening the fridge. "I'm going to fucking vomit!"

"Do you want me to help you?" I called from the bathroom. I'd launched an attack on a viciously ringed bathtub.

"Nope, I got it."

Silence.

"For the fucking love of PETE!" he hollered. "I'm going to DIE!"

"Are you sure you don't want me to give you a hand?"

"Nope. No problem. Almost done."

He'd brought a radio along to save us from having to engage in any real conversation with each other. The station played random but recognizable songs. Virgil sang along here and there, and I noticed an odd consistency is his lyric alterations.

* * *

"Layla" by Eric Clapton:
"Layla, you got me in my ASS,
Layla, I'm beggin' darlin' please
Layla, darlin' won't you lick my hairy AAAA-AAASS."

* * *

"Lollipop" by the Chordettes:
"Lollipop lollipop
Oh lolli lolli ASS
Lollipop lollipop
Oh lolli lolli ASS."

* * *

"Landslide" by Fleetwood Mac:
"I took my love . . . in the ASS
Climbed the mountain of your ASS
And I saw my reflection in the crack of your ASS
A landslide came out of your ASS."

* * *

Virgil has been doing this for so long, making "ass" the ending of at least every other line, that it requires no conscious effort on his part. And the funny thing is, he's not that bad of a singer. That's my brother-in-law.

If my husband and I did have children, would Uncle Virgil babysit them? Would I come home to find him rocking a baby to sleep, singing "Twinkle, Twinkle, Little Ass"? How scarred would they be after overhearing a discussion of granny porn? And would that discussion permanently damage their relationship with their grandparents? Would their grandparents teach them how to make a balslamic marianade for substance, and dwelve into other such snidbits? If we didn't have kids, we wouldn't have to find out.

* * *

CHAPTER 3

Puppy Love

My mother indulged me as a child when it came to pets. Hamsters and guinea pigs lived in our care at times, but we *always* had hermit crabs. They're low maintenance, easy to dispose of when dead, and all around good pets, aside from when they manage to clamp down on the delicate piece of skin between your thumb and forefinger, as my very favorite crab, Hermie, once managed to do.

I remember the shocking pain of Hermie's pinch and reflexively jerking my hand, sending the little bugger flying across the room and hitting the wall like a flung marble. With instant remorse, I ran to him, or her, I'm not sure how you tell.

"Are you okay, Hermie?" I asked.

He came through undamaged, but I put him next to Crabby, his roommate and my second-favorite crab, for comfort. The idea of a favorite hermit crab is, to the adult me, illogical. I can think of no other combination of words less affectionate than "hermit" and "crab." It's not as if he cuddled with me, or did tricks, or was physically more endearing than the others. A hermit crab is a hermit crab.

A friend and fellow nerd in the neighborhood had hermit crabs as well. She often brought her hermit crabs over to play with my hermit crabs. Truth be told, hermit crabs don't really play. They are idle and silent, curled up tight in their shells, or frantically climbing around and silent, ostensibly searching for the beach from which they were crab-napped.

On weekends we set up obstacle courses for our hermit crabs. Rarely was there a winner. More often we just stared at them, willing them to come out of their shells and race through cardboard tubes and A-framed textbooks. If one of our beloved crustaceans did participate in our maze, it could take six or seven hours to complete.

We stopped having hermit crab races when one of the participants disappeared. He must have taken a wayward crab-walk when we took a break. Bored with the lack of action, we'd adjourn to the kitchen for the occasional snack of high-fructose corn syrup or melted cheese. The race took place in a near-empty, sunken room, and the only place he could have gone was through an opening around the pedal of an old electric organ, which was literally the only item in the room.

We called to the little guy (I guess all hermit crabs seemed male to me) to no avail. We placed a capful of water and a pellet of hermit crab food at the opening, but we never saw him again. Perhaps we'd have had better luck with different bait, like high-fructose corn syrup or melted cheese. If I had to live on water and pellets, I'd want to crawl into a hole and die, too. I don't know what happened to the organ, but I'm sure his remains are still in there, lonesome shell and dust.

I cannot fathom why we had an electric organ or how it came to be in our possession. No one played it. Mine was not a musical household.

As an adult, I engaged my mother in a series of disjointed and incoherent phone messages, trying to solve the riddle of the organ.

"Hi, Mom, it's me. Remember when we had that organ when I was young? Why did we have that? Where did it come from? Call me if you think of any details."

"Hi, Mandy. I can't imagine what you mean by *organ*. I think you might be confused. Are you talking about an instrument? Let me know."

"Hi, Mom. *Of course* I'm talking about an instrument. It was an electric organ, like a piano. We had it in the townhouse, the first place we lived that was decent. Remember? Call me."

"Hi, Mandy. I can promise you that we never had an organ. Are you drinking? And I find the comment about the townhouse being the first decent place we lived a tad dramatic. Talk to you soon."

"Hi, Mom. Are you forgetting that we lived in a barn? I'm loading my gun."

Whenever my mother forgets something, I tell her that I'm loading my gun. This is in response to her emphatic and lifelong request that if she goes senile, I should take her into the back-yard and shoot her.

"Hi, Mandy, I figured it out! When you were really little, our neighbors down the street had a pipe organ. And the guy could play the *heck* out of that thing. Is that what you're talking about? And you can put down the shotgun; it was an apartment *converted* from a barn. Call me."

"Hi, Mom. Got your message. No, that's not what I'm talking about. Never mind. I'll talk to you later."

"Hi, Mandy. I can tell you that we absolutely never had an organ. Ever. Call me."

I started to believe my mother then. I *wanted* to believe her. If I'd fabricated the organ, maybe I'd also made up the hermit crab. Maybe I could free my conscience from guilt over the lost pet that had been weighing me down. But then, my mom left one final message.

"Hi, Mandy. Load the shotgun. I kind of remember the organ now. I don't remember why we had it, where it came from, or what happened to it. I hope that's helpful."

* * *

If a person's ability to care for pets is any indication of her parenting skills, I had yet another reason to avoid motherhood. From my experience with hermit crabs alone, I feared throwing my child across the room or losing them within the depths of an instrument of questioned existence.

Hermit crabs were the point of embarkation on a long journey of poorly executed attempts at pet ownership. Mike and I made the classic mistake of assuming that the seasoned ages of twenty and twenty-one brought with them the responsibility necessary to care for pets. First it was Rita, an adopted cat. She started as the perfect feline, but when we took in Puck, a second cat, Rita became a demon in gray fur. At the time when we acquired both cats, we lived in a two-bedroom apartment, the normal sort in a complex where you hear the intimate sounds of your neighbors' highs and lows, the fighting, the fucking, and the occasional vomiting. The apartment was comfortable, except for the fact that we were broke, couldn't afford the rent, and there is nothing more *un*comfortable than asking a relative for money.

We moved on to a small, wonderfully cheap, and unfortunately leaky boat. The adventure could not negate the fact that moving two cats onto a thirty-foot vessel of compromised construction is not a great idea.

In addition to our unhappy felines, we had to contend with John, who lived on the neighboring boat. I remember tiptoeing down the dock on the way to our boat, trying in vain to quell the creaks of wet wooden planks, but John held a position of perpetual lookout.

"Hey, guys." He appeared from nowhere. "You should know the Coast Guard has a raid scheduled." I studied the large lesions on his head and concluded that they did not bode well for his overall health.

"Really?" Mike asked. "You think the Coast Guard is going to conduct a raid of the Benicia marina?"

"Yeah, the government's been watching me. So, if I disappear, you know something's up."

"Uh-huh." Mike hurried me onto our vessel.

"Can I hug your wife?" John asked.

"What?" I said.

"No," Mike answered, "you cannot hug my wife."

"Okay. Permission to come aboard?"

"Permission denied," Mike answered.

"Okay. Well, I got you guys a Thanksgiving present."

"Oh dear." Mike sighed.

John produced an enormous can of yams that had expired

three years prior. He was delusional, but I believe he had a good heart.

Rita took off within the first two weeks of our moving to the boat. I like to think that she found a doting old lady living in one of the overpriced condos overlooking the marina. Not the type to have too many cats, or the kind who tries to harness a cat and take it for walks, but a sweet little widow named Ruthie who wears pearls every day and springs for Fancy Feast. Puck, relieved by Rita's departure, spent the next three months huddled in between stacks of sweatshirts until we came to our senses and moved back to dry land.

Living again within the comforts of drywall and an uncompromised roof, we found ourselves with an opening for a new pet.

Mike wanted a dog.

"I just don't think we're ready," I said. "We need to do some more work on the house first." We were living in a fixer, and I feared bringing a rambunctious puppy into the construction zone that we called home.

"It's like having kids," Mike said. "There's never going to be a perfect time."

"What do you mean by that?" I asked.

"What?"

"Why did you compare it to kids?"

"I don't know," he said. "That's one of those things that people say about pets and kids."

"But we're not having kids," I said.

"Agreed. So let's get a dog."

This was the first tick of the clock. I knew that a biological clock was a metaphor but still assumed that if I had one, I would hear an actual ticking emanate from deep inside my body when it one day started. Instead of a "tick," it sounded more like "let's get a dog." The ticking continued when we named her, agreeing that we couldn't call her by any name that we might one day want to use for a child. We named her Jody. Tick. Tock.

I must have had few responsibilities and a sparse social calendar, because I spent a ridiculous chunk of every day doting on this animal. I took her swimming and to the dog park, kept her well-groomed, and cooked her chicken and rice when she was ill from eating too much feces or some other such dog malady. I became a dog person and naïvely thought I would always be so.

Mike and I drove home one afternoon, having taken Jody for a swim in the Carquinez Strait, when we saw a sign for an estate sale. Odd artwork, boxes of ancient books, and other random and alluring items cluttered the lawn. We pulled over and left Jody in the car. A two-minute tour through the home revealed all manner of dark intrigue. Behind the amateur, semi-pornographic artwork, I discovered a set of Soviet film posters, which I then purchased. Another scavenger loudly announced that a chocolate Lab appeared in distress in the back of a Subaru. Before I considered the welfare of my dog, it struck me that I'd become someone who owned a chocolate Lab and a Subaru. "Oh, barf," I muttered.

"All of the windows are rolled up, and it's really hot outside," she continued.

Everyone looked around.

"That's my dog and my car," I fessed up. "But she's fine."

"Well, she sure is panting heavily," the woman declared.

The crowd stared, collectively contemplating what the

temperature would have to be to fry an egg or a dog's brain. Blood rushed to my head; the walls pulsed with judgment.

"She's panting because I just took her swimming, and up until a minute ago, I had the air-conditioning on in the car, so she's fine," I snapped.

My anger doubled, because I worried she was right. I found Mike in another room, unaware of the scene.

"We have to leave," I said.

"Okay." He continued browsing an assortment of eccentric hats.

"No, we're not looking at the accessories of the dead," I said. "We have to leave right now."

"Okay, okay. Calm down."

Our departure was ostensibly the result of a horrible and nosy person making an unfounded accusation. In reality, it was because I was too mortified to remain there. When we got in the car (it wasn't hot and Jody was fine), I cried.

Having been called out felt like assurance that I would be a horrible parent. Then again, how many times had I been left in a potentially hot car as a child? Or a running car, kidnapper-ready, outside the bank or the 7-Eleven?

"Stay here. I'll just be a minute." That was the standard line my mom used before exiting the vehicle. Sometimes she'd add, "Don't touch anything," and glance nervously at the parking brake, which made me want to touch it. The keys would be in the ignition, and I'd be sitting in the front seat. Car seats were not yet conceived, and the vehicle may or may not have had seatbelts. If it did, we didn't use them. But no one kidnapped me, and I was too much of a pussy to release the brake.

Aside from that one lapse in judgment and the public reprimand that ensured it would never happen again, I was a good owner to Jody while we had her, but then Mike was offered a job overseas.

"Well, that's great," I said, "but we can't move overseas. We have a dog."

"So you think we should turn down this opportunity because we have a dog?" he delicately asked.

"Well," I countered, "she's our responsibility."

"Amanda," he said in his you-must-be-high voice, "we've been offered a chance to travel the world, to leave our shitty, miserable jobs. We're not turning that down because we have a dog."

I eventually agreed that foregoing this opportunity for our dog was not logical, at least not for selfish bastards like us. Friends watched both Jody and Puck for a year, and the job continued, so both animals were re-homed, adopted by people we knew, who happened to be better parents and responsible adults. Still, my former pets gazed at me, sad-eyed and shivering, in my dreams. I swore then, no more pets.

Of course, I swear all the time regarding living things in my charge, but with conviction that dwindles over time. My assertion to *Not Have Pets* included the fine print: *Except for the Occasional Labrador*. This was a good indication regarding my feelings on motherhood, as well. My insistence that I would *Not Have Children* tick-tocked its way to *I Will Not Have Children Yet* before ringing an alarm that sounded a hell of a lot like *Let's Make Babies!*

* * *

CHAPTER 4

I Like My Ovaries Frozen

As a teenager, I completed a study abroad program in Russia. My lessons were focused equally on the language and the national drink. In addition to those studies, the natives did their best to educate me on why I would not be able to have children. The first was a woman who spat at my feet because I was smoking. Then she cursed at me, something about a mother's duty. I was sixteen years old at the time with no intention of having children or sex. Well, maybe sex, but definitely not kids. I was also in reasonably good shape; it's not as if I had a potbelly sticking out that could have been mistaken for a growing fetus. The woman, on the other hand, looked to be about twelve thousand years old, and because of this, I was unable to react with anything other than stunned amusement. I got the impression that she would spit upon any female caught smoking, no matter their age or condition.

The other instance when a native of the Motherland told me I would never be able to have children was when I sat down on a concrete step. I was chatting with friends outside of an apartment building and took a seat. One of my friends, also a female teenager, instantly began pulling at my arm to get me to stand up.

"Amanda, what are you doing!?" she gasped. "Stand up!"

"Why?" I stood and looked at the seat of my pants, expecting to find that I'd rested my derriere on a wad of gum or the decaying carcass of a small animal.

"The concrete is cold, and your ovaries will freeze," she warned. "You'll never be able to have children."

"You're joking," I said, sitting back down.

"No, she's right," another friend chimed in. "It happened to my aunt."

I imagined scores of sterile Russian women blaming themselves for having sat on concrete or smoked cigarettes. All Russian men are virile, of course.

Russia taught me to be skeptical of superstitions, and further travels to Micronesia introduced me to the absurdity of folklore. It started with a trip to jail. I was working in Palau as the buyer for a television show, and learned that Palauan legends are depicted via carvings, otherwise known as storyboards, which are a popular item among the tourists. I'd seen some impressive storyboards for sale at souvenir shops but had also heard from the locals that the best place to buy a storyboard was at the jail, as the inmates have time aplenty to perfect their carving skills.

Entering the Koror jail felt as casual as walking into a dentist's office in a strip mall. There was no barbed wire or metal detector to pass through. I guess law enforcement can afford to be a bit more lax with security when the prison is on an island. Escape options are limited.

The storyboards cluttered a tiny room in between the front office and the inmates' living and recreation areas. The doors were open. This meant that if I wanted to look at the storyboards, I would have to do so while being studied by the prisoners peering at me through the doorway. I felt slightly reassured by the fact that they appeared terrified by me. This was good, as there was no guard standing there with a stun gun, or a baton, or even Mace. In fact, there was no guard at all, just one meek and soft-spoken inmate who had somehow earned the privilege of working the storyboard room.

I couldn't commit to a purchase that day and ended up returning on four subsequent occasions. The inmates, who take notice of any female presence in the facility, grew bolder with each visit. Some would even venture into the storyboard room while I was there.

"I'm James," a burly, tattooed man said.

I've never been able to decline a hand extended for a shake, but I should definitely learn to do so.

"Hi, I'm Amanda. Nice to meet you." I shook his hand and realized that this was not a mere handshake but more of an opportunity for James to have contact, though limited, with the bare skin of a female. He held on with no intention of releasing me.

"How are you?" he asked, leaning in way past my personal boundaries of you're-too-fucking-close.

"I'm well, thanks," I said.

"No," he said. "How *are* you?"

It occurred to me then that "How are you?" was really code for something else. Maybe he was asking me if I wanted cocaine, or if I had any cocaine, or if I wanted my storyboard hollowed out and filled with some other kind of narcotic. Maybe he wanted to know if I trafficked in small rodents or had a letter to deliver to him from his long-lost love. Whatever the subtext was, I couldn't decipher it. I was too busy trying to communicate my own subtext, which was: *Let go of my hand right now or I will kick you in the balls.*

After I extracted myself, but before I retrieved the hand-sanitizing lotion from my purse, I chastised myself for relying on subtext and not delivering the merited kick.

When I eventually bought a storyboard, I received with it a written copy of some of the legends these carvings depict. This is when I learned of the particularly gruesome Palauan legend involving the magical spider that showed people how to have a vaginal birth (as if the vagina doesn't show you on its own how to have a baby, whether you're ready for it or not). As the legend goes, before the magical spider came, Palauans delivered all babies by Cesarean, unaware of the existence of the birth canal and that the vagina is actually an appropriate exit for a baby to take. And I'm not talking about modern Cesarean, whereby an incision is made, the baby retrieved, and the mother sewn back up. Rather, the mother was knifed open, the baby removed, and the mom left for dead. This always led me to wonder who was raising the babies, because it sure as hell wasn't the fathers. If the Palauans could have thrown a little Russian wisdom into their culture, I'm sure that all Palauan women would have been chain-smoking and sitting on concrete for hours at a time.

Modern Palauan women survive only because a spider, disguised as a young man, came to Ngiwal from the island of Pelilieu. He took a bride, promptly impregnated her, and nine months later held off the knife-wielding village women (notice the murdering idiots are women) and supervised the first natural childbirth. From then on, Palauans halted their practice of butchering women in labor.

As gruesome and illogical as this legend may be (haven't women been having babies naturally since . . . always?), what continually trips me up is that the man was really a spider taking the form of a man. Why? And let's face it, it wouldn't really be a *man* who figured out this ingenious little anatomical tidbit, would it?

If you bought a carving depicting the first natural childbirth, it was likely to show a recently deceased woman on one side, to represent the old manner of delivery, and in another section a woman giving birth, guarded by a man. This couple will be threatened by a group of villagers with spears and knives. Luckily, the storyboard artists didn't spend too much time on re-creating the details of birth. There was no etching out of placentas and umbilical cords, but they loved to carve women's bare breasts. It was hard to find a storyboard for sale that didn't depict at least two sets of nipples. The artists were imprisoned men, so maybe that was to be expected.

Other legends were equally weird. One of the most popular involved a couple who meets on an island to spend the night "staring into each other's eyes." I admit that every now and then, Mike and I stare into each other's eyes, but usually this leads to other things; we certainly have never spent an entire night like this. At some point during their staring contest, a turtle makes off with the girl's grass skirt (apparently this was *naked* staring, which makes me think that they may not have been entirely focused on each other's eyes, after all). Somehow this leads to the realization that the egg-laying cycles of turtles relate to the phases of the moon, thereby assisting Palauans in their turtle-hunting endeavors.

Another Palauan legend concerned a fish-bearing breadfruit tree. Without ruining the excitement of this one, I can reveal that it ends with corpses floating throughout the flooded town. You can see why carvings of these legends make wonderful gifts. Then again, they are no more gruesome than the Bible.

* * *

Palauan pregnancy stories left me mystified, but I found an equal lack of logic among my peers in the United States.

Friend: "So, we're going to start trying to have a baby."

Me: "Congratulations!"

Friend: "Thanks!"

Me: "What made him decide he's ready?"

Friend: Blank stare.

Me: "You guys *did* talk about it?"

Friend: "Well, not really."

Me: "What do you mean?"

Friend: "I just went off birth control."

Me: "Did you tell him?"

Friend: "Yes, but he doesn't think we're ready."

Me: "But you're going off birth control anyway?"

Friend: "Well, it's not really up to him; it's my body."

Me: "So, since you're the one who's going to have stretch marks, you get to decide that he's going to father a child?"

Friend: "Well, we're married. We're going to have kids at some point. I'm just deciding that now is the time."

Me: "You know, he could end up with stretch marks, too. Lots of guys get crazy fat during their wives' pregnancies."

Friend: "Yeah, that argument isn't really swaying me."

Me: "I had to try."

Friend: "Why don't you want me to have a baby?"

Me: "It's not that I don't want you to have a baby!"

Friend: "You think I'll be a crappy mom?"

Me: "Of course not. We both know that I'll be way crappier as a mom than you. I just want you both to be ready."

Friend: "You're right. You will be a crappier mom than me."

Me: "You don't have to be so agreeable."

Luckily, she did not get pregnant between the time of that conversation and when they actually divorced. Of all the marriages I've been exposed to in my life, the majority of them were temporary situations, as opposed to the "till death do us part" variety, so I've always struggled with the thinking that marriage could give one person the power to make a life decision for the other. I mistakenly thought the let's-bring-a-child-into-the-world issue had to be unanimously agreed upon, which in my mind has little to do with whether or not the couple has a piece of paper declaring them wed.

I remember being shocked by the fact that Mike's parents, now my in-laws, were married. The idea of someone whose parents were married seemed odd to me.

"So, what do you mean, your parents are married?" I asked Mike in the early days of our relationship.

"What do you mean, 'what do I mean'? They're married, husband and wife."

"They're married to each other?"

"Of course. Who else would they be married to?"

"Huh. So, did they divorce somewhere along the way and then remarry?" I asked.

"No. They married when they were very young, and they *stayed* married."

"Wow," I said. "The whole time?"

It was good that we had this conversation early, as it gave Mike a fair indication of the type of girl with which he was getting involved.

"You are one screwed-up chick," he said.

My goal is to never have to incorporate tactics into my marriage. One woman bragged to me about going off birth control, waiting until her husband started to get frisky, and then saying, "By the way, honey, I stopped taking the pill." Offering up this information to her spouse just as he started dry humping her leg was not exactly fair. By waiting until he had a gigantic hard-on, she got what she wanted. He said "okay," and they had imminent conception.

I had other, equally confusing conversations with girlfriends of mine. They went like this:

Friend: "I think I might be pregnant."

Me: "Wow, congratulations! Did you take a test?"

Friend: "No."

Me: "You didn't take a pregnancy test?"

Friend: "No."

Me: "Why not?"

Friend: "I don't know."

Me: "Well, let's go get one!"

Friend: "No, I don't want to take one yet."

Me: "What!?"

This was where my first bout of complete confusion clobbered me. I could not fathom suspecting pregnancy without immediately heading to the nearest drugstore to pee on a stick and know for sure. The rest of the conversation continued to baffle me.

Me: "I didn't know you guys were trying."

Friend: "Oh, we're not."

Me: "Wait, you're on birth control?"

Friend: "No."

Me: "You're not on birth control?"

Friend: "No."

Me: "But you have sex?"

Friend: "Yes."

Me: "Then you're trying to get pregnant."

Friend: "No."

At this point, we stared at each other blankly for a moment.

Me: "If you have sex, and you don't use birth control, then you're basically trying to get pregnant."

Friend: "Well, we're not really *trying*."

Me: "Huh. Let's get a taco."

Many women think that you're trying to get pregnant only if you're charting your ovulation and consuming mass quantities of folic acid and screwing at certain times of day and with optimum body temperature, whatever that may be. Others are shocked when they get pregnant, despite the fact that they haven't used birth control, as if not wanting to be pregnant will magically keep it from happening.

Aside from magical spiders and frozen ovaries, the absolute craziest piece of advice I've ever heard about conception is this: "If you want to get pregnant, you shouldn't be drinking."

Since the first glorious fermentation in the history of time, alcohol has assisted in getting women pregnant, whether they want to be or not. Alcohol makes people want to be naked, which is a step in the right direction toward making a baby. I know you should be the picture of health and blahdy-blah, but let's be real. When I eventually embarked on pregnancy, I had to all but slaughter two of my first loves, alcohol and nicotine. I agree that women should not be throwing back martinis throughout gestation, but the idea that alcohol at the time of conception will have ill effects on the future child is just one more seed of irrational guilt planted in the minds of women. And I don't fucking buy it. I fiercely harbor the hunch that you can sit on concrete, smoke a pack of cigarettes, get liquored up, and still someday be a fantastic parent.

My rules for conception are as follows: Do not have contact with old Russian women. Do not consult legends or folklore from any society. Make sure husband wants baby, not just sex. Beyond that, how hard could it be?

* * *

CHAPTER 5

A Walk in the Park

Mike and I reached a point of feeling settled. Not in a bad way, like when the ice in your cocktail melts and the vodka separates from the grapefruit juice and settles into something you no longer want to drink. Not that kind of settled. That's cocktail neglect and it's a terrible waste. Don't do it.

We were settled in a good way. We were through with life on leaky boats and temporary jobs overseas. We lived in a house (this time a thankfully habitable one that didn't require massive repair work). Finances were tenuous but not terrifying. Most important, we were in agreement and emotionally ready to start a family. Many discussions led up to this, in which we'd analyze the parenting techniques of people with demon children, in homes where the primary form of communication was screaming, and contrast those with families in which all family members appeared to genuinely like each other. Members of those families talked to each other like humans should talk to each other, communicating without an excess of eye-rolling and passive-aggressive behavior. They seemed to enjoy their house-holds, rather than view them as battlefields. These distinctions were important to us. We knew it wouldn't be a cakewalk, but we felt that if we were at least on the same team, we could keep our living room from turning into World War III. Obviously, we had parenting all figured out; it was time to get knocked up.

Six months after throwing the birth control pills in the trash, I was pregnant (yay!), but I miscarried soon after (boo!). Nothing cures grief quite like a Labrador, so I reneged (again) on the previous No Pet proclamation, and we adopted Betty. It took us a while to name her, which was a good indication of our failure to bond with her. Calling her "Miscarriage" or "Emotional Filler" just didn't seem right.

She was a good companion when I eventually became pregnant again, and we took long walks together. She'd pee on things, and I'd waddle slowly after her, trying not to pee myself.

Near the end of my pregnancy, a squirrel-killing epidemic swept through Boise. Squirrels became ill and died in unnatural numbers. The virus went unidentified, and Idahoans treaded on a lurking panic that it might mutate into a human plague. For Betty, the squirrel affliction was ecstasy.

We crossed through the park one afternoon and spotted a squirrel near the base of a tree. Betty broke free and sprinted for it. I didn't think much of it; she chased squirrels all the time. This squirrel had caught the plague, though, and was ill and slow to escape. Betty clamped down on the animal, joyfully shook her head around, and threw it up in the air. The squirrel landed and began trying to drag itself to the tree with a lone front paw, like a wounded soldier dependent on only one working limb. At the same time, it made a high-pitched screaming noise that I didn't know squirrels could make. Betty pounced again.

"Betty, no!" I yelled, but presented with the prospect of a barely live squirrel to play with, I had no sway. She threw the squirrel around, chewed on it, and shook it, all while the squirrel keened, which undoubtedly made it more fun for Betty. Maybe that's why they make dog toys squeak, to simulate the cries of wounded prey.

With my enormous belly, I tackled Betty. It took ten minutes to pin her under me and get the squirrel out of reach. It was instinct to try to stop the situation, but the squirrel was still alive. The more humane act would have been to let Betty finish it off. We stopped traffic a few times as I dragged her home. There's nothing quite as eye-catching as an energized Labrador and a pregnant lady smothered in diseased squirrel blood. This issue is not addressed in *What to Expect When You're Expecting*.

A week later, with squirrels still expiring long before their due date, Mike and I had friends over for dinner. From outside, Betty clawed at the sliding glass door, asking for entry. I opened the door, and she proudly walked into the middle of the dining room and dropped a dead squirrel at my feet, as if not wanting to show up to a dinner party empty-handed. Shrieking ensued from both me and our guests. Mike came running from the kitchen.

"What happened?" he asked.

"Betty just brought us a present," I said. I ordered Betty back outside while our guests peered at the squirrel, flat and encrusted with dirt.

"Ew," Mike said with a cringe. He looked at me, hoping I'd offer to remove the corpse.

"Oh, no you don't!" I said. "*I* kill all of the bugs, *I* dealt with the last squirrel incident, and *I'm eight months' pregnant!* You need to *man up* on this one!"

"Okay, okay."

These little dramas seemed good for us. We were confronted with unexpected situations and dealt with them as necessary. Betty was parenting prep and we were doing *awesome*. Surely I'd been too hard on myself during the I'm-not-fit-to-be-a-pet-owner phase.

Then the baby arrived, and with her came the cliché of a pet turning into a chore. We walked her less and bitched about her more (the dog, not the baby). Her companionship and affection fell short when compared to her shedding and demands for attention. Mike and I once again became the reason people put bumper stickers on their cars that read: "A dog is for life, not just for Christmas."

Virgil moved to Boise with space in his life for an animal. He took ownership of Betty and gave her the attention she deserved. They were perfect for each other, not least of all because of their similar standards of hygiene. Then came the phone call.

"Hello?"

"Oh my God."

"Virgil?"

"I don't know what to do."

He was crying. I'd only ever known Virgil to cry when intoxicated, when mass quantities of hard alcohol amplify every real and imagined emotion. This is a condition I may have experienced myself, once or twice.

The tears, combined with his words, set my mind thinking. Whatever the situation was, it would likely include jail, if he wasn't there already. He was probably calling to ask me to bail him out. I'd never bailed someone out of jail before; the prospect was slightly exhilarating. How much did that sort of thing cost? Should I hit the ATM, or did jail accept credit cards? Where was the jail, anyway?

"The first thing you need to do is sober up. If they don't have you already, turn yourself in. Is this your one phone call, like in the movies? Where are you?"

"I'm at the Humane Society."

"Oh, no. You didn't try and release all the animals, did you? Are you trapped in a dog kennel?"

"It's Betty," he said.

"I'm not going to get to bail anyone out of jail, am I?" I asked with a hint of disappointment.

"I need to put her down. They have you on record as her owner and need your permission." He detailed Betty's condition for me before turning the phone over to a volunteer. I gave my consent for Betty's destruction and cried. I cried for Betty, for Virgil, and because Betty's demise was surely related to having been in my care. I had no doubt I was the world's worst pet owner. I hoped that wouldn't translate to the world's worst parent.

"Mike, these animals are killing me," I whined.

"Actually, I think it's the other way around," he said, then deftly ducked to avoid the shoe I threw at his head.

"I'm serious. We can never have another animal. We have to agree on this."

"Agreed."

"But what about our kids? They're going to want a pet at some point."

"Fine," he said. "We'll give them invisible pets."

"Our kids are going to be gifted, so of course they'll never buy it."

"You're right," he reasoned.

"What if we give them a plant first, and they can only graduate to a pet if they can first keep the plant alive for a year?"

"Are you going to secretly water it with bleach?"

"I'll try not to."

"And what happens when they keep the plant alive for a year? What do we get them then?"

"A fish," I answered. "A single, easily flushable fish."

* * *

CHAPTER 6

I'm Not Having Twins, Bitch

As much distress as I felt about our pets and what they indicated about my abilities as a caregiver, that discomfort paled in comparison to what it is like being pregnant. Yes, it's normal and natural and all of that, but let's not dismiss that it's also *growing a human inside of you*. It's a damn miracle—a painful, embarrassing, and awkward miracle.

"I'm so excited!" I said, as Mike and I headed to an early ultrasound appointment.

"Me, too," he replied, but I thought he looked a little pale. We were a few months into pregnancy, so this was a frequent look for him.

"You know, we're not going to the gynecologist. We're just going to get an ultrasound," I assured him.

"Why would you say that? I don't have a problem with the gynecologist."

"Mike, it's okay. You're a man. You're allowed to be a little afraid."

"What? Me? Afraid? Don't be silly, I *love* the gynecologist!" he protested.

Mutterings and mumblings regarding the various doctors Mike is *not* afraid of accompanied the rest of the drive.

Only in movies had we caught sight of this medical unicorn called the ultrasound. A doctor would move a device resembling a remote control over my pregnant belly, and we'd first lay eyes on our budding offspring in grainy, black-and-white images. I pictured the little tyke giving us a wave, or the finger.

After I donned the hospital gown, we waited for the ultrasound tech. The clinical feel of the room reminded me of the Digestive Diseases branch of the National Institutes of Health where my mother worked for years, a place where research doctors compared notes on the most humane way to dispatch a guinea pig, injection versus a quick snap of the neck.

The tech entered with a casual greeting and pulled out what appeared to be a twelve-inch dildo.

"Holy crap, what are you going to do with *that*?" I asked.

"This is the wand we use for the vaginal ultrasound," he informed us.

"That's not a wand," I corrected him. "A wand is thin and used by fairies and magicians. That thing is a *probe*."

"Don't worry," he assured me, "this is only going to be inserted an inch or two."

"It's *huge*," Mike remarked.

"You're not helping," I said.

The tech fitted the probe with a condom and began slathering it with KY.

"Wait!" I said. "I'm not ready." Both the tech and Mike stared at me, awaiting explanation. "No foreplay?"

My attempt to lighten the mood made an awkward situation worse.

"Sorry. I'll be quiet," I said. "I was just kidding," I continued. "I'm ready. Really, I'll shut up now. Go ahead, *probe* me."

I struggle with mildly uncomfortable interactions, preferring for them to be either completely comfortable or catastrophic. My determination to turn the ultrasound into a disaster succeeded.

Of all the wisdom that mothers impart on the newly pregnant, I cannot fathom why no one warned me about the probe. Physically, it was entirely endurable. Visually, it was a terrifying and violating image. I would have appreciated a warning. Instead, veterans offer up such pearls as, "Your stomach is going to get huge," or "Just wait until you can't even find your ankles anymore; it's really gross."

Hollywood is no greater help. The movies show only the external ultrasound. They omit the large sheet draped over the genital area and the technician's arm disappearing under that sheet, with both prober and probee craning their necks at the screen, pretending that actual penetration isn't occurring. The reality also requires, if the tech is male, a token female to be in the room, a hospital employee there to guard against any later allegations of misconduct and subsequent lawsuits. Having that other person in the room makes it even more awkward, because I don't know to whom I should direct my inane and meaningless comments about the weather. If I exclude Token Female from the conversation, she might think I'm rude, but if I speak to her, I have to look across the tent formed by my knees, and I don't want either of them to think I'm trying to watch, because that would completely break the unspoken rule of pretending that penetration isn't actually occurring. It's best to alternate between wrenching your neck to get a view of the monitor and, when you can't do that any longer because your neck will surely snap, which can't be good for the baby, just staring at the ceiling and announcing to the room at large, "It sure is *windy* today!"

* * *

In the first trimester, I did not notice any expansion in my butt, but I *did* notice that my underwear inexplicably receded. One day, it simply failed to fully cover my crack. I mentioned this to my husband.

"You know what?" I said. "I was thinking that my underwear shrank, but really I've put some pounds on my butt."

"Oh, yes," he replied, "your butt has *definitely* gotten bigger."

His immediate and emphatic answer, confirming the ballooning of my backside, was ice water on my ego.

"Well, excuse my *fat ass*."

The butt enlargement caught me off guard. Sure, I expected my belly to get big, but I didn't pay any attention to my rear. Before I knew it, my office chair was mysteriously hugging my hips. And why should the derriere need to increase anyway?

There was, however, a consolation prize that went along with being pregnant: It was the first time since prepuberty that I didn't have to suck in my belly. I've heard a dozen women cite this as one of the biggest perks of pregnancy, other than getting a real live baby out of the deal. And I certainly didn't wait until my belly actually grew to start letting it all hang out. Once I knew I was expecting, I felt free to undo the top button of my jeans, relax, and breathe a long sigh of relief. It was my right.

Another one of my newfound rights was to freely and

frequently tell people to "shut the hell up!" Blame the hormones, but also the sobriety. Studies show that forced sobriety is a direct cause of bitchiness in pregnant women. The time in our life when we are not allowed to booze it up is the time when we need booze the most.

The bitch persona can't entirely be faulted to the incubator. Men often experience a time of unprecedented selfishness and poor judgment in the six months before and after the baby is born. It's panic over fatherhood and frustration that their sex life suffers, along with a marked decrease in their wife's over-all hotness. This results in the unfortunate condition of Asshole. The husband (Asshole) doesn't have the same alcohol restrictions as his pregnant wife, which he exploits fully to the point of cruelty, thereby enhancing in her the aforementioned bitchiness, which may inspire him to drink further. It's a vicious cycle.

"Shut the hell up," came in especially handy when people started instructing me in things like the manner in which I should give birth to my baby, whether or not I should work, whether or not I should breastfeed, and how to raise my child in general.

Another useful phrase is "Back the fuck away!" which I found particularly applicable when people felt entitled to put their hands on me.

Pregnant me: "Excuse me, could you please tell me which aisle has the hemorrhoid cream?"

Grocery store lady: "Oh!" She began rubbing both hands up and down my belly. "Is it a boy or a girl?"

Me: "Please stop touching me."

Grocery store lady: "You're carrying low. That means it's a boy." Her hands moved in circles on either side of my abdomen.

Me: "I am ordering you to step away from the belly."

Grocery store lady: "Have you been dreaming of lemons? You should drink parsnip tea."

Me: "Are you fucking kidding me?"

Grocery store lady: "Make sure your dream catcher is correctly placed."

Me: "Cease and desist!" By then I felt downright fondled.

Grocery store lady: "Let me call Pat from the meat department; she's right about guessing gender nearly 50 percent of the time."

Me: "BACK THE FUCK AWAY!"

Grocery store lady gasped and recoiled in horror.

Me: "And where did you say the hemorrhoid cream is?"

When it came down to it, I felt I should be awarded a medal for managing any measure of kindness during my pregnancy. My inner bitch trampled decorum, not only in response to hormones and reluctant sobriety, but also fatigue. "Fatigue" doesn't come close to describing what I felt, but I can't find a synonym that's brutal enough. It's the sort of tired that allowed me to fall asleep on wet concrete, to find myself snoring while completely awake, or drooling midsentence. A purgatory of consciousness. My eyes were mere slits, my cheeks (among other parts) sagged heavily, and my face hung as a wilted, blotchy version of the cheerful, radiant me that lived in my mind's eye. This zombie state is inevitable when a body toils at creating another human. Women should not apologize for finding it difficult to attain any level of politeness during pregnancy. We get through it as best we can, trying not to murder anyone.

In my third trimester, an unshakeable fever accosted me,

and I ended up in the maternity ward in the middle of the night for an evaluation and to make sure the baby was still alive, kicking, and functional. With my husband dutifully in tow, a nurse led me to a private room. She opened the bathroom door and pointed out the gown hanging on a hook.

"Obviously, you'll take everything off, and here's your gown." I nodded understanding. "And you know how to give us a clean catch?"

"Uh . . ." I stared at her dumbly. Were we going to engage in some sort of sport to start off? To monitor my reflexes or agility, perhaps? A game of catch to really get that baby's heart rate up and going?

"Here's a wipe," the nurse explained. "Use two, from front to back, and then urinate the first part in the toilet, then in the cup—"

"Oh yes," I cut her off, "I know how to pee in a cup." Urinating into a receptacle held a solid position on my résumé; I just hadn't been familiar with the term "clean catch." But really, peeing in a cup when nine months' pregnant is easier said than done. That far along, I had absolutely zero view of myself down south, and as a female, I was already limited in my capacity to direct a stream. Inevitably, I peed a great deal on my arm and hand while furiously waving the cup back and forth beneath me, hoping to catch enough for whatever tests needed to be run. Luckily, they don't need much. If they did need more, I'd have to pee again within ten minutes anyway. I did my best.

"Well, that's an interesting way to wear the gown!" the nurse cheerfully proclaimed upon her return. Translation: *You're an idiot!*

"Oh, did I do it wrong?"

In my misguided logic, I thought they'd want the opening in the front so they could access my belly. But who needs an opening in a gown when you can just hike the whole thing up to expose both my belly and my hoo-hoo? In addition, I soon discovered that the actual front of the gown was riddled with slits and openings to gain access to the nude me underneath.

When properly dressed, in bed, IVed, and belted with both fetal and contraction monitors, the nurse left us alone. And then I had to pee again. My husband helped unhook me and carted my IV bag along as the large contraption-that-was-me made its way to the bathroom. I lifted my gown, sat on the toilet, looked up at Mike, and warned, "I may have to toot." This was immediately followed by the long, loud, and unmistakable sound of my passing gas into the toilet basin, and the resultant, unending echo.

"I'm sorry. There's no way to do this"—I gestured to the whole, inglorious, and pregnant me—"and still be cool."

"Honey," he assured me, "you stopped being cool a long time ago."

The nurse reappeared, this time wearing a facial mask, to properly hook me back up to various machines. The mask was disconcerting. Had my passing of gas been audible outside of the private room? All the way down at the nurses' station? Was she protecting herself against my possible olfactory offensiveness?

"So, I hear you were diagnosed with swine flu last week?"

"Um, no, that wasn't me," I corrected.

"Okay, then!" She smiled and left again.

Mike and I tried to piece together how this rumor could have started. We failed.

"It seems," she explained when she returned, still masked, "that last week we had another lady in with swine flu, so we'd like to test you for it just to be sure."

"All right."

"So, I'll just need to take a swab."

"Okay." I pictured a Q-tip making the rounds just inside my nostril, or perhaps scraping the inside of my cheek, at worst a brief gagging as she swabbed the back of my throat.

"But you're really not going to like this," she added.

"Why?"

"Well, it's not really a swab."

"What is it?"

"It's more like a wire with a little itty bit of cotton at the end."

"Ouch."

"And I have to insert it all the way up into your nasal passage," she pointed to her eyeball, "until it starts to bend," she curled her pointed finger.

"Whoa."

"And then I have to press it there and rub it around."

"Wow." I took a deep breath.

"And I have to do it for thirty seconds."

"Holy crap." I braced myself.

"And I have to do it on both sides."

"Oh, *come on*, lady! Are you finished? Is that it? Is there anything else you want to add? Let me guess, you have to wax my butt and give me an enema at the same time, just so I don't get too comfortable, right? *Right?*"

"Honey, calm down," my husband instructed.

I refrained from further outbursts, resigning myself to the experience. Better to get it over with than to dwell in fear on what might not be as bad as imagined.

Awe of the sensation ate through the first ten seconds. Echoes of my grunts and gasps bounced off the walls. My eyes streamed, and while I allowed the rest of my body to squirm, I obediently kept my head motionless. My desire to be cooperative was not for the nurse's benefit, but because I wanted to make sure we got this on the first take. I also didn't want to take any chance of the swab accidentally lodging in my brain or poking out of my eyeball.

When thirty seconds came to an end, the nurse removed the swab, and I laughed uncontrollably. This was the laughter of shock. Mike and the nurse exchanged cautious glances. Through my hysterics, I tried to explain, "You can't imagine how unbelievably *horrible* that was! That was worse than my wildest dreams!" More maniacal laughing followed.

When I regained composure, the nurse tackled the second side. By the end of this thirty-second period, there was no laughter. I was sobbing. It is the only time in my adult life that a purely physical pain has left me crying like a child. It's true, labor hurts, but I'd rather go through ten hours of labor than another ten seconds with wires up my nose.

Two hours later, the nurse entered the room sans mask.

"Good news!" she proclaimed.

"I don't have swine flu?" I ventured.

"You don't have swine flu. So, we're going to give you some Tylenol and send you home."

"Thank you," I said.

"Yes, thank you," Mike echoed.

The gratitude was genuine, of course, and intended as thanks for ensuring that my unborn baby was in good health, but it seemed an odd thing to say, like thanking a proctologist after an exam. When we got to the car, I paused and looked at my husband.

"Did I really just thank her for shoving wires up my nose?" I asked.

"Yeah," he confirmed, "we both did."

* * *

I miraculously made it through two pregnancies without pickling either of my children in the womb, yielding two healthy babies. Emilia was first, followed by Ivy two years later. Emilia was a very prompt child and as a result was born exactly on her due date, which happened to be Memorial Day. This proved problematic. On the day of her actual birth, the hospital was understaffed because of the holiday. It seems odd to short-staff a maternity ward on a holiday. It's not as if fetuses recognize these days as not conducive to birth and thereby delay their entrances. A newborn has no regard for a three-day weekend.

Complications, coupled with doctors who could not be located, led to frantic nurses screaming, *"Get one of the ER doctors in here NOW!"* Not exactly what you want to hear as first-time parents in the delivery room. Emilia was thankfully fine, despite or maybe because of the use of forceps during her delivery.

We'd reached some sort of crisis point when the doctor looked at me and said, "I need to know right now, if it comes down to it, do you want forceps or a C-section?"

A margarita was not one of the options, so I answered, "Uh . . . forceps?"

If she'd shown me the forceps when she asked the question, I would have opted for a C-section. I pictured forceps as oversized tongs, or perhaps a slightly larger than normal metal shoehorn, something to give the little tyke a push. Forceps were, instead, an enormous pair of interlocking, medieval instruments brought into the room in a large, menacing black bag.

"You must have mistakenly grabbed those from the Tower of London," I said. "I'm trying to give birth; I think the Torture Ward is down the hall."

I'm not complaining, as I got a healthy, albeit slightly indented baby out of the deal.

I experienced the joys of C-section during Ivy's birth, so I don't feel like I missed out, procedurally speaking. While Emilia is a punctual child, Ivy is a stubborn one. She refused to assume the correct position before birth and thus had to be removed by Cesarean. The visual horrors of this procedure make forceps look like lollipops.

It doesn't matter how you give birth; either way, you're probably going to need stitches. The only good thing about being fat as a new mom is that you usually can't see the carnage beyond your belly, which I wrongly assumed would return to a normal size after giving birth. Not having a visual of the repair work that happens in your far southern regions is a good thing.

With a Cesarean section, the gore regrettably lurks in plain view. When the doctor said she would be using staples, I pictured something akin to the staples I use at work, the type I employ when stapling three pages of what should be a ten-page report. I'm counting on the binding of the document to make up for its content insufficiencies.

It turns out that more serious hardware (think Frankenstein) is needed when you're trying to close a baby-sized opening in the abdomen. Even that would have been fine, had one of my staples not been cockeyed. Perhaps I'm just finicky, but when someone in the medical profession closes a wound or gash on my body, I'm in favor of it being completely closed, as opposed to *sort of* closed or *almost* closed. I'd like the internal me to stay there and out of sight.

Medical indignities extend beyond pregnancy, of course, and I'm sad to report that mole removal does not garner the sympathy I feel I deserve when undergoing anything that involves stitches. I gained a little more compassion when the doctor went back a second time to remove an additional chunk of tissue at the site of the former mole. Not only did I have a bigger wound to showcase, but also a bigger possibility of death by cancer. If cancer is my demise, I hope it originates from the mole and not my lungs. Ex-smokers statistically receive 50 percent less sympathy than those who die by cancer not born of their own vice.

After my abnormal mole was removed, the dermatologist closed the wound with dissolvable internal stitches. But my internal stitches then decided they wanted to grow up to be external stitches, and I hit the jackpot as far as the ick factor goes.

"Honey, will you take a look at my incision?" The mole had been removed from my upper back, where it was difficult for me to see. "I think there's something going on back there." Mike agreed to check it out, because we are married and he had no choice.

"It's an internal stitch growing out of your back," he said.

"What?! Ew!"

"Do you want me to pull on it a little?" he asked.

"No!"

"Do you want me to trim it down?"

"No!"

At the first opportunity, I went back to the doctor's office, where a nurse pulled on the stitch a little before trimming it down. It's startling the first time it happens, but as the next seven stitches emerged to greet the world over the following two weeks, the novelty wore off. Dissolvable, my ass. The resulting scar is much bigger than it would have been if the internal stitches had dissolved as they were told to do. We tell our children that it's Mommy's gunshot wound.

My mother wins the award for all-time goriest, most-sympathy-inducing injury and subsequent treatment. In one of her less graceful moments, she fell head over heels down a long flight of wooden stairs. The bones of one hand were in such a state of disarray that they required the assistance of an external fixator to put them back in line. This is a medieval contraption of bolts, rods, and lengths of metal. The rods are drilled into the bone and extend out through the skin. A length of metal with periodic ball-and-socket joints connects the rods sticking out of the limb. It's genius and pure nastiness all rolled into one, as you can see the rods where they enter and exit the body, reminiscent of Clive Barker's *Hellraiser*.

"Hi, Mom, how's it going?" I asked over the phone, from three thousand miles away.

"I think I'm going to have to enter the Betty Ford Center when this is all said and done. The amount of painkillers I'm on is *ridiculous*."

We laughed, both knowing that painkillers needn't be factored in for either of us to be good candidates for the Betty Ford Center.

"When you get the fixator taken off, are you going to keep it?" I asked. I pictured it as a family heirloom, something I'd someday pass on to one of my daughters, should they share my gruesome fascination.

"Are you kidding? *Of course*, I'm going to keep it. It's creepy, and I earned it." Through the fog of pain pills, I heard a hint of pride.

* * *

After the births of both of my daughters, I was given prescriptions for pain medications, which I seldom used. I'm just not a pill person. Mike, on the other hand, suffers from a bad back, thrown out of whack years ago. He's tried chiropractors, yoga, surgery, inversion tables, and contraptions purchased from late-night infomercials. All to no avail. He's been known to be fine for three months running and then spend two months sleeping upright or not at all. The biggest perk to us having children was, of course, the children, but a close second for Mike were the medications I was prescribed. When I went into labor on both occasions, Mike's coaching had less to do with the act of giving birth, and more with reminding me to accept all of the prescriptions offered. I've appalled him in the past by declining drugs and have vowed, as a tenet of marriage, never to do so again.

* * *

CHAPTER 7

Life of Crime

Like all new moms, I had a baby and then decided that I should smoke pot for the first time. I had to reach both my early thirties *and* motherhood before deciding that I could partake in a bit of marijuana without any danger of it leading to a severe heroin problem. Before then, I held little doubt that smoking pot would inevitably turn me into a crack whore in no time. Self-control and moderation have never been my strong suits.

People dismiss the gateway drug theory as ridiculous, because everyone knows plenty of people who smoke pot regularly but have never moved on to stronger fare. But that's not the way I saw it. It was more like this: I bet you'd be hard-pressed to find a crack or heroin addict who's never smoked pot. Plus, I'd grown up in the eighties with Nancy Reagan telling me to just say "no." Nancy Reagan seemed impossibly old to me, and saying "yes" to drugs would have been like the unforgivable Disobeying of Elders. For me, that was one of the worst sins a kid could commit, and it would lead to something really awful, like a parent forcing you to look them in the eye as they tell you how much you've disappointed them. If my mother or father had ever told me they were disappointed in me, I very well might have jumped off a bridge, knowing that my failure in life was complete.

Luckily, I grew up and learned that sometimes your elders are senile and that worrying about disappointing your parents is a colossal waste of time. *Of course* you're going to disappoint them. That's part of your job. And the appearance of things like laugh lines and sun spots convinced me that I'd matured enough to handle a little light recreational drug use. Smoking pot was a rite of passage I'd missed out on, and I wanted to catch up with the rest of society. I needed experience to back up whatever it was I'd tell my children someday about why they should or should not smoke marijuana. I had also, by that point, let go of my dream of one day being a Secret Agent, so a toke or two wouldn't ruin my chance of acceptance into Secret Agent School.

Mike and I flew to Southern Baja, to a community largely comprised of retired, expatriated, former hippies, none of whom would be offended by that description. At least, I don't *think* they'd be offended. They are, by nature, laid back with a healthy sense of humor, and they're usually stoned in any case.

On a Friday night, we left three-month-old Emilia in the mostly capable hands of Mike's parents, without telling them about the full extent of our plans for the evening. After a few beers (this was my first of many mistakes) at the home of a couple with whom we were close friends, we embarked upon the event of my first high. Nothing happened, nothing changed, and I began to ponder why anyone would be so enthusiastic about smoking pot, much less spend money on it. What on earth was the big deal? I thought back on every instance in which I'd been in the company of stoners, and I started to wonder if they hadn't just been putting on an elaborate ruse. What if smoking pot and getting high was really a worldwide game of pretend that I wasn't in on? What if being baked was akin to telling the stark-naked emperor how dashing he looked in his new getup? Or were such questions just the beginning of the infamous and dreaded paranoia? No, there was definitely something I was missing. I recalled a conversation with a friend of mine who'd been downright appalled at my abstinence from marijuana.

"*What?!* You don't smoke pot? *Why?*" His anger was startling. I had to remind myself that we were talking about something that was technically illegal. His tone would have made more sense if he'd been chastising me for not recycling.

"Um, I don't know," I replied. "I get addicted to everything I try."

"Pot isn't *addictive*. I've smoked pot *every day since I was fourteen*, and I'm not addicted." Statements of such intelligence and vehemence assured me that I simply hadn't yet reached a true high.

Another friend of mine smokes pot a handful of times throughout the year, always preceding her high with the same statement: "Normally I don't like pot at all, but this is really nice." I chew on my lips, dying to tell her how many times she's uttered this obvious falsehood through the course of our friendship, but that would highlight the prudishness I'm so desperately trying to mask.

A particular expat joined the group later in the evening, and he happened to be in possession of significantly stronger weed.

Tall and slight, with square-framed glasses and thinning hair, he was a perceptive man whose company I could only describe as comforting. The cadence and tone of his speech were soothing, never hurried, and welcoming. That's how I should have approached his offering, in an unhurried manner, but I was a cigarette smoker with the finesse of a frat boy, so I sucked down the joint as if it were a Marlboro. Then, after a lifetime of walking the stock straight and very narrow, I finally experienced a high. It was goofy, odd, and silly. For a time.

"Your turn, Amanda."

I looked across the table to our hostess. We were in the midst of a card game, and I suddenly felt very off.

"Amanda?"

"Um . . ."

"Are you okay?"

"Um . . ."

"Uh-oh," she said.

"I don't feel very good." I put my cards facedown on the table, naïvely assuming I'd be returning to them, and made a desperate sprint for the bathroom. With what limited coordination I could muster, I propelled myself to the WC and into the proper position over the commode before I threw up.

Reality broke down into a series of frames flashing in quarter-time . . .

I close the bathroom door . . .

I lift the lid to the toilet seat . . .

I position my head over welcoming porcelain . . .

I open my mouth . . .

And nothing comes out. Well, not exactly nothing. I didn't throw up. Instead, I crapped my pants.

"Shit!"

I looked at myself in the mirror, and staring back at me were three unwelcome acquaintances: Disbelief, Shock, and Surprise. This is the expression that automatically registers on the face of any adult who has just crapped her pants.

"Shit! Shit! Shit!"

And then I did throw up, with unbelievable force.

This was the smallest bathroom on the planet, about two square feet, probably designed and constructed by someone who does not take up or require much space. Perhaps a midget who has had two of his limbs amputated.

I momentarily stopped throwing up and delicately dropped my pants to survey the damage. Luckily we were talking about a very small amount of matter, amazingly contained by the brand-new Playboy G-string my husband had purchased for me, paid too much for, and was no doubt looking forward to seeing me in later that evening. My jeans were clean and miraculously immune from the chaos that had taken place within their confines. And then I had to poop again. There was no time to try to push my undies down, so I sat on the toilet and quickly yanked the G-string to one side. My body emptied itself, with absolutely no say on my part. I began throwing up again. Because the bathroom was two square feet, I was able to reach the cabinet under the sink, where I found a plastic bag full of candles. Our friends kept candles hidden all over their house, always in reserve, the way most people approach toilet paper. I dumped the candles into the sink, and vomited into the bag repeatedly while my bowels voided, very much in sync with the vomiting. The plastic bag had holes in it, never having been intended for such purposes.

Eventually, graciously, there was nothing left to leave my body. I took stock of the situation. The first task before me was to remove the once sexy, now offensive G-string from my person. These were not breakaway panties, which I now see the benefit of, so I couldn't remove the garment without first removing my jeans. I couldn't take off my jeans without soaking them in the rising tide of vomit on the floor, steadily leaking through the bottom of my compromised receptacle. I decided I would have to physically rip the G-string off. I wasn't sure if this would even be possible. An image flashed through my mind of the Incredible Hulk in a thong: bulging green muscles, throbbing veins, and pink lace. Thankfully, I was able to tear the fabric; it turns out G-strings aren't all that well constructed. Had it been made of chain mail, I still think I could have done it, because embarrassment of that magnitude equals superhuman strength.

I heard a soft knock on the door.

"Hello?" whispered a female voice.

My candle-loving friend had come to check on me. A quick glance reassured me that at least the vomit hadn't started leaking out under the door. I opened it a millimeter, afraid that she would see the chaos of bodily output, or smell it.

"So, how's it going?"

"Great," I answered.

"Are you okay?" she asked.

"Nope. No. Well, yes. I mean, I wasn't, but I'm okay now."

"Well, what can I do?"

"I need cleaning supplies, all of them." The gravity in my voice told her not to inquire further about my well-being, not to offer to help, not to do anything other than bring me all of her household cleaning supplies. "And a trash bag."

The last thing I would have wanted at that moment was for my husband to see me in such a ridiculous, pathetic, and unhygienic state. At the same time, I wondered why he hadn't come looking for me. Wasn't he worried? Or at least curious what I was up to? I had been gone from the group for quite some time. But this is why women prize their friends so dearly, because we know they'll come check on us, hold our hair back if we need it, and make sure there isn't any vomit crusted to our cheeks before we rejoin the group and pretend everything is fine. And, when the situation calls for it, they will procure cleaning supplies.

I told no one, of course. And I cleaned as never before, determined to erase all evidence, one particle at a time. When I was finished, the bathroom shined. I tied the trash bag tight, so that it was completely sealed. I wanted to ensure that the contents— vomit, paper towels, and the remains of my underwear—would never come into contact with light or air or another human being. It occurred to me then that I might have to account for the whereabouts of the G-string, my husband's gift, at some point, but the subject mercifully never came up.

"You doing okay?" Mike asked on the way home.

"Yeah, I'm fine."

"You were gone for a long time."

"Yeah, I wasn't feeling too good."

"I'm sorry, sweetie," he said.

"I think I'll jump in the shower before bed."

"Good idea," he replied. "That'll make you feel better."

The next day, we returned to the scene of my crime. I was relieved when we pulled up to the house to find that the neighborhood's stray dogs hadn't gotten into the trash overnight, which is a regular occurrence. Would I be able to play it off if a mutt trotted by, ecstatic as only dogs can be, with a small and slightly stained but clearly-identifiable-as-former-panties piece of fabric dangling from its mouth?

When this fear receded, I replaced it with panic that my friend would ask why her bathroom smelled of sewage, or why she'd found a shredded G-string in her trash. But I'd covered my tracks well.

"I don't know what exactly went on in there last night," she said, "but thank you, our bathroom has never been so *clean*!"

"Thanks for having us over," I said, hoping not to dwell on the subject of the bathroom and the secrets it now held.

"We should do it again sometime," Mike suggested.

"Ugh," I muttered with an involuntary cringe.

He shot me a look, questioning why I would be so rude in the face of our close friends.

"Yeah," I corrected myself. "Do you guys have plans tonight?"

Maybe I should have just smoked pot in my teens like everyone else I knew. No one wants to get on a bike for the first time in middle age. That's what it felt like. I could have killed the mystique of it early on and saved myself the later embarrassment, or gotten the embarrassment over with at the appropriate age, during the mortifying eternity that is puberty.

Or perhaps I should have stuck to my guns, continued on the path of a strictly legal life, and trusted in my instinct to abstain. The truth is I didn't want to be left out; my ego couldn't stomach the thought. It turns out I'm not immune to peer pressure after all; it just hits me about fifteen years after the fact. I've smoked pot a handful of times since Mexico, less potent product without disastrous results, but never with a concrete enjoyment. Marijuana is only wasted on me.

There is something to be said for accepting what is not for you. This doesn't always come easy. In fact, I'm really atrocious at this. And I equally fail at accepting that, even though something is not right for me, it may be just fine for other people. After all, not everyone who smokes pot craps their pants. At least, I'm pretty sure.

* * *

CHAPTER 8

Police Escort

I used to work in the butter room of my husband's real estate brokerage. In the back of the business, one office had bright yellow walls, in contrast to the more moderate tan of the other work areas. It became known as the butter room.

Despite the joys of parenthood, I was relieved when Emilia first started going to day care and I could return to work. Some would say that makes me an asshole, but that's just because they're assholes. Not everyone has the inherent wiring to be a stay-at-home mom, and in terms of that wiring, I fall into the deficient category.

I anticipated that my job would continue as it had prechildren. Unfortunately, we found ourselves in need of a secretary. I am not a people person. I prefer hiding back in the butter room, churning out advertising blurbs and getting crunchy with numbers. I am the worst possible candidate for a secretarial position.

"What would you think about sitting up front?" Mike asked.

"I would think 'no.'"

"Really?" The disappointment was evident in his voice; I knew guilt was on its way.

"Truly," I confirmed.

"It would be really helpful to have someone at the reception desk."

"Then I wish you much luck there."

"Come on, please?"

"I hate people. I don't like dealing with them," I reasoned.

"That's not true."

"Yes, it is. It would be socially irresponsible of you to put me into direct contact with the general public."

Despite the validity of my arguments, I knew I'd give in. When it comes down to it, I am madly in love with my husband and will do whatever he wants.

"You won't even have to answer the phone," he promised. "We just need someone to take up space up front."

"Well, gosh, if you're going to flatter me . . ." I relented.

"Thank you!"

"I am not answering the phone," I stated.

"That's fine. No phones."

Over the next few months, my husband slyly added secretarial duties to my to-do list. He'd become annoyed if I failed to answer the phone, though I reminded him on numerous occasions and in the bitchiest of tones that he'd specifically promised me a blanket exemption from any and all phone responsibilities.

The phone rang.

Mike: "Are you going to get that?"

Me: "Nope. I don't do phones."

Mike: "*Please* pick up that call. It's important."

Me: "I don't want to."

Mike: "Hurry! Before it goes to voice mail!"

Whenever someone yells at me to "*hurry*," I am overcome with panic. The task at hand becomes life-or-death crucial, as if I have to disarm a bomb, and I freak out under the pressure.

Me: "*Fine!* Hello, this is Amanda." Pause. "I'm sorry, but Mike is unavailable at the moment. Can I take a message?"

Mike: "What?! I'm available! I'm right here! I need to take that call!" This was accompanied by Mike jumping up and down in front of me, furiously waving his arms to get my attention. I pretended not to see or hear him.

Me: "I'll give him the message. Have a great day."

Click.

Mike: "Why would you *do* that?"

Me: "You told me to answer the phone."

Mike: "But I needed to talk to him."

Me: "Then why didn't *you* answer the phone?"

Mike: "Because you're supposed to screen the calls first."

Me: "But you knew who it was, and you knew you wanted to talk to him. You just like the idea of having a secretary, don't you?"

Mike: *Sigh.*

Me: "You better go call him back. It sounded urgent."

Mike: "If you weren't my wife, I would fire you."

Me: "I know."

I actually wanted to be fired. Every now and then, I'd threaten to leave the business and make gobs of money elsewhere, enough that he could hire a real receptionist. To date, however, the government has yet to offer me a five-hundred-thousand-dollar-per-year spy job.

When I was young, I was enamored with the idea of said spy job. In my vision of adulthood, I would wear slightly sexy but mostly professional business suits, carry around an attaché case, and live in a small but posh apartment in DC. I wouldn't have any pets or plants, because the government would send me to Europe on frequent intelligence missions of incalculable importance to our nation's safety. That forecast didn't pan out.

Mike and I have been married nearly two decades. We have two daughters, a dozen houseplants, and an occasionally cared-for vegetable garden. We live in a split-level in Idaho. How did I end up in Idaho? I swore I'd never be landlocked, having always lived near a bay—Chesapeake or San Francisco—and honestly, I don't even *like* potatoes. I have a gym membership and an aesthetician, and I look up casserole recipes on the Internet. Where on earth is my attaché case?

There are traces of the younger me, of course. I have tattoos and fuck-me boots, and while I'm obviously not a good stoner, I haven't lost the ability to create a respectable hangover. But despite my vices and dependence on day care, I took to motherhood better than anyone who knows me would have expected. My children elicit patience from me that I do not afford the general public, likely *because* of day care. I adapted so well that I started to question whether there was anything more to me beyond the roles of wife and mother.

The weighty word "career" even floated around in my head. But what to do? It seemed that almost every female I knew was in the same predicament, the what-am-I-doing-with-my-life stage. Why couldn't I have chosen something and just done it? Study something, like marine biology, and then embark upon a long and rewarding career working with injured or orphaned dolphins? Think of the benefit I could now be providing to the underwater community, had I gone that route.

As indispensable as I was in my husband's business (when one overlooked my telephone inadequacies), I didn't feel that he considered me to be actually *working*.

Mike: "So, I had this great idea for a new business. You want to hear about it?"

Me: "I'd love to, but I'm really in a hurry right now."

Mike: "What do you have to do?"

Me: "I've got to get to the post office to mail a certified letter to a deadbeat tenant, swing by the bank to make some deposits, pick up a case of paper from the office supply store, then get to the office, process the payroll, clean the bathrooms, and write the ads you asked for."

Mike: "Yeah, but there's nothing you *have* to do."

Me: "Excuse me?"

Mike: "It's not like you have anything that *has* to be done right now."

This statement and my stint as a receptionist were two of many indicators that our ability to work productively together had run its course. My front-desk presence turned into a daily challenge to make it to five o'clock without telling anyone to fuck off, which turned out to be much more difficult than I'd thought.

While I sat one day staring at the phone, willing it not to ring and contemplating sabotaging it, a solicitor walked in. He was a salesman for security systems. I am not, at heart, antisalespeople. I've been there. I sold vacuum cleaners door to door for a whopping five days before I decided I couldn't take any more doors slammed in my face.

Towering and bulky, the salesman effectively employed his size to intimidate. He leaned over my desk; I slouched down in my chair. Calluses covered his enormous hands. A threatening air about him suggested that if I didn't buy a security system . . . well, who knew what could happen?

I cowered for a minute or two as he worked through his spiel. And then the ridiculousness of the situation hit me. I straightened up, and with the change in my posture, I saw a change in his. I put on my best don't-fuck-with-me face.

"Don't fuck with me!" I screamed. Then I clenched the mechanical pencil in my hand, brought it high over my head, and slammed it down, impaling his hand and pinning him to my desk. He wailed like a little boy, begging for mercy I didn't have. No, wait, that part didn't happen.

"If you'd like to leave your card," I said, "that would be fine."

"Well, you talk to your boss, little girl, and I'll be back to check in on you," he threatened, though I never saw him again. That's probably a good thing, as few terms of endearment cultivate my inner bitch quite like "little girl."

A different salesman from a competing company tried the same tactics on me at my home. He attempted to scare me into handing over my credit card with phrases such as, "I'm sure you're aware of what's been happening on your street," and "A gal like yourself wants to make sure her family's safe."

I was holding Ivy at the time; she was just an infant on my hip. The salesman was already planning in his head how he'd spend his commission, most likely on rims and a subwoofer, or perhaps a penis pump. He was shocked that I wasn't an easy sale. But the truth is, I *was* interested. You can't watch as many documentaries on serial killers and Bill Kurtis productions as I have and not contemplate purchasing a security system at some point. However, I refuse to respond to fear and intimidation as sales tactics, which is why I now have fifteen baseball bats strategically placed in my home, as opposed to a legitimate security system. In my daydream regarding this salesman, instead of impaling him with a writing utensil, I have a Taser at hand.

"Check it out," I say. "I already *have* a security system."

Then I zap the bastard, and he flies back onto my front lawn, crumpled and moaning. My daughters look on, clapping with delight. "Do it again, Mommy!" they cheer. "Do it again!"

My reaction to these men convinced me that if I was going to embark on a new career, a sales position was not a good fit. Something that involved weaponry, however, might be my calling.

I'd majored in Russian in college, which was in line with my goal of working for the government on secretive and dangerous missions. I longed to be Clarice Starling, to have Anthony Hopkins whisper my name in a voice both creepy and enticing. In a search for my current identity, these dreams resurfaced, and for a few days, the FBI was *absolutely* the path I would take; *nothing* could stop me. A few days later, I was over it. Not only would the FBI Academy take me away from my family for an excruciatingly extended period of time (turns out I *do* have feelings, after all), but if I actually made it through, we would then be at the mercy of the Bureau's placement, and they currently do not have any field offices in Idaho. We were too rooted to consider moving for my silly little career in counterintelligence.

I decided to look at things on a smaller scale. I could be a police detective. *That's it*, I thought. *That's my calling, and nothing will stop me*. I applied for a police ride-along, downloaded an application, watched countless hours of *The First 48* on the treadmill, and started doing pull-ups. Sure, I'd have to be a patrol officer for a few years and work my way up, but I knew I could do it.

Any apprehensions I harbored about police work had nothing to do with confrontation or criminals or shooting people or getting shot. It was about much more terrifying possibilities, such as being forced to ride a bike. While I have many talents, riding a bike is not one of them, and few scenarios sound as humiliating as a bike cop crashing all over town.

My fascination with law enforcement wasn't entirely born of cop shows and detective novels; it began at a very young age with an obsession over crime, a shock at the elements of society that prompted the need for law enforcement. The first time my friend Nora came to my house after school, I showed her my collection of articles.

"Look at these," I said, pulling out an old briefcase my father had given me (my parents did a great job of fulfilling my nerd wish list). I opened it to reveal hundreds of newspaper clippings, a veritable best-of from the paper's Metro section, marinating in the long-lost smell of my father's cherry tobacco.

"What are these?" she asked.

"I collect these," I explained. "They're all about crime."

"That's . . . creepy," she said.

"Yeah," I agreed. "Look at this one! It's about this guy who flipped out and decapitated his son along the side of the road."

"Oh. Wow. That's really awful."

There's nothing like a good decapitation story to cement the bonds of friendship.

I spent a week filling out an application to the Boise Police Department, which required listing comprehensive information regarding every aspect of my life, ever. I called friends and acquaintances to get their complete contact info, warn them that they might be interviewed regarding my character, and encourage them not to disclose how often I make jokes about finding dead hookers in hotel rooms. I tried desperately to recall the dates surrounding my residency and work history over the previous ten years, and I realized with slight dismay that these histories showed a startling lack of stability. There were dozens of questions along the lines of, "Have you ever murdered anyone?" I answered "no" with 99 percent confidence.

Pages of the application dedicated themselves to prior drug use, along with the repeated warning that applicants would be subjected to a polygraph test. I could read between the lines. The message was: You'd better just fess up.

I always prided myself on the fact that I'd never done any illegal drugs. That is, of course, until my brief and unfortunate south-of-the-border encounter with marijuana. Having been such a straight arrow all of my life, the fact that I had once smoked pot didn't seem like a deal breaker. Surely not all police officers were marijuana virgins, and they'd probably smoked more weed than I had.

I was honest.

The application asked for dates, circumstances, and number of times used. I thought about the circumstances and decided to say "Vacation in Mexico," not "Shat myself."

I was honest.

I'm not a very good liar, and with the threat of a polygraph, there was no way I would even try.

So, I was honest.

I made a copy of my application and sent it to the Boise Police Department. Everyone I knew told me I was the perfect candidate. I couldn't fail.

After my application was received, I got a call from the BPD. I anticipated scheduling an interview. In my head, I was already decked out in police gear; in my husband's head too, though his vision was one of a more sexual nature, with some key items of clothing absent, like pants.

"Is this Amanda?"

"Yes!"

"I'm so sorry if you were misled about the process," she said. "You have to take a standardized test before your application will be reviewed."

"Oh, okay," I said.

"You can look up the dates and testing sites on the Internet. I'll go ahead and keep your application here, and then it's already filled out and on file when you complete the standardized test."

Mike and I spent the next hour discussing whether I would wait for the upcoming local test date or fly to Seattle to expedite the process. We also talked about how our lives would change in terms of parental responsibilities. He would have to be more flexible with his schedule. He knew and accepted this, realizing that if I was in a position of some importance and responsibility, he was the parent that day care would call when one of our children spontaneously threw up and needed to go home. He would be Mr. Mom when Mommy had to work odd hours catching bad guys. That was the plan.

The phone rang again, a different lady this time, also an

employee of the Boise Police Department.

"Is this Amanda Turner?" Her voice was less hearts-and-flowers than the previous lady.

"Yes," I answered.

"I have your application here."

"Okay."

"You did the one thing that automatically disqualifies you."

"What's that?" I thought she was joking. What on earth could *disqualify* me?

"You smoked marijuana."

"Oh. But I thought . . . I mean . . ."

"You can't smoke marijuana and then decide a few months later that you want to be in law enforcement." I could see her point. There was a definite bite to her voice, and I was glad we weren't having the conversation face to face. I'd gone from almost-a-cop to established criminal. "You can apply again in three years," she informed me.

"I thought . . ."

"What?" Her annoyance was poorly masked.

"I mean . . ." I stuttered, confirming that I was, indeed, a card-carrying idiot.

What I had *thought* was that if I was honest, my single indiscretion would be forgiven. Did I not get extra points for making it through my teens and twenties completely ganja free? It turns out that the answer to this is no, you do not get extra points. Pot probably would have been forgivable if it had been in my younger years. Apparently, once you're all grown up and reclaiming your childhood dream of a career in law enforcement, you should know better.

"You thought what?" she demanded.

What I had *thought* was that any police department would immediately recognize how fantastic and dynamic I was and what an indispensable asset I would be to The Force.

"Nothing," I said. There would be no attaché case in my life. Only casseroles. "Nothing."

Thus ended my career in law enforcement.

* * *

CHAPTER 9

Do As I Say, Not As I Do

Assuming my children could survive the early years, I was mortified by the thought that they would one day go through the barely survivable stage of life between ages fifteen and twenty-five. Aside from the peril they'd put themselves in during this treacherous decade, they would also have to contend with whack-jobs. College is often the first instance when people have to deal with whack-jobs on their own, without parents there to intervene.

At my college freshman orientation, I randomly offered those around me Pez. I happened to have Pez in my purse, dispenser and all. Maybe I thought it was a good networking tool for college, and I offered it to those seated next to me as a gesture of goodwill.

"Hey, would you like some Pez?" The intended subtext was: *We're in this together, I don't know anyone either, let's all relax and be friends and break the ice.*

The girl to my left politely declined. The guy to my right

accepted the Pez but misread the subtext. I didn't know it at the time, but my offering had just rewarded me with a stalker. He wasn't a total lunatic, never approaching me with weapons or small animal sacrifices, but he definitely crossed the line of what is acceptable social interaction. Following me home from class, standing in the hallway outside of my dorm room, he'd wait for my next emergence.

"I have to study now," I'd call through the door, "so I'm going to be a couple of hours." Silence. "So, why don't you go ahead and leave," I'd suggest, staring at him through the peephole. And there he'd stand, still as a post, looking back at the door.

"That's okay," he'd say. "I'll just wait here."

People thought it was funny, a little puppy dog following me around. When you're the one being followed, it's not funny; it's just creepy.

It took a while for others to see what I saw, but eventually they did, and the student in charge of keeping the peace on our floor realized that I wasn't using the term "stalker" loosely; I was using it correctly. He spoke with my admirer, using phrases like "charges of harassment," and my stalker drifted off.

I don't know what became of him, and the question looms: Did his behavior continue, and if so, did it escalate into something dangerous? Maybe he got help: counseling, drugs, a hobby. Whatever became of *him*, I know *I* changed from the experience. If I sense the latching on, the unhealthy attachment, the lack of self-awareness, my claws come out. I'd rather be seen as a callous bitch than ever have another stalker.

As adept as I am at being a horrific asshole to ward off threats, it's not enough when I imagine my children in the same scenario.

The Mother Bear instinct kicks in; I can easily picture ripping out the throat of anyone who dared stalk one of my daughters. Lord help their future suitors, as well. I'll be an unapologetic nightmare of a mother-in-law.

My first college roommate (I'll call her Skankella) and I shared a dorm room for a semester. The room was thick with clues as to how things would work out with Skankella. When I arrived a few days before classes began, she had come and gone, leaving a note on the bed. Friendly phrases like, "sorry I missed you," and "can't wait to meet you," mingled with telltale signs that should have clued me in, like "my boyfriend and I will be working the Renaissance fair," and "PS - I was here first, so I took the bed by the window." When she finally showed up, she was accompanied by the boyfriend. They say that you can't judge a book by its cover. I'm sorry, but sometimes you can.

Skankella and Pigstopher, the boyfriend, arrived late the night before classes started. After all the required and blatantly false utterances of "It's so nice to meet you," the pleading began.

"Is it okay if Pigstopher stays the night?" she asked.

I didn't like Pigstopher, not one bit, not from the first moment I met him. He was friendly enough, but he was a thirty-year-old man dating a seventeen-year-old. The same people who say that you can't judge a book by its cover also like to say that age doesn't matter. But sometimes it does. An adult over the age of twenty-five dating a teenager is a flag engulfed in flames. And, I'm pretty sure, illegal.

"Gosh, Skankella, I don't know." I was such a wimp. She knew she had me.

"Oh, please! It's just so far for him to drive."

"Um . . ."

"I promise we won't do anything!"

"Well . . ."

"*Please?*"

Pushover, I consented.

There I was, lying in bed and staring at cinderblocks painted with a soft yellow hue, in my conservative, toddler-esque pajama set, thinking of the advent of my academic life and the very important career I would embark upon as a result, when I began to hear a soft mewing from the bed that was four feet from mine. *This is not happening*, I told myself. The noises increased, including the *OHs* and unmistakable suction sounds that accompany the frenzied probing of a body cavity. She neared climax; deep moans stepped up in pitch. I turned from the cinderblocks and sat bolt upright in bed.

"Get the *fuck* out of my room. Get the fuck *out* of my room. Get the *fuck out of my room.*"

Ironic, in hindsight, that my semantics were so dead on; I literally wanted the *fuck* out of my room. Pigstopher put his clothes on in the dark and slipped out without a word.

Our relationship deteriorated from there.

"Hi, Skankella." I had returned from class to find her sitting at a small card table we kept in our room, a bottle of grain alcohol and shot glass in front of her.

"Hi, Amanda. Hey, thanks for doing my laundry."

"I didn't have much choice, Skankella. It smelled really bad."

"Yeah, sorry."

"If it gets bad again, and you don't do it, I'm going to throw it away."

"No, I'll do it," she promised.

"Great. That would be just great."

"So, I had an appointment with Health Services today." My heart went out to the staff in the tiny trailer that served as the campus medical facility.

"Yeah? What for?"

"I have genital warts," she said.

"You know, you don't need to tell me these things."

"Sure I do! You're my roommate! Want to hear about how they diagnose genital warts?" she asked.

"No."

I also had the unfortunate experience of seeing Pigstopher's testicles, though not close enough to note the absence or presence of warts, due to a large hole in the crotch of his jeans. This vision occurred after they had hastily dressed post-coitus when I showed up unexpectedly to our dorm room in the middle of the day. This was before texting; otherwise she could have warned me that they were going for a little Afternoon Delight.

For someone who has diligently worked to be a coldhearted bitch, it is amazing how long I let the ridiculous situation with Skankella limp along, because I didn't want to hurt her feelings. I could have, and rightfully should have, demanded a new living situation after that first night, but I gave in time and time again, because she didn't have many friends. I won't be able to protect my kids from roommates like Skankella, but I can work to make sure that my girls do not grow up to be Skankellas themselves. I think that's a reasonable goal for any parent to have.

More frightening than the whack-jobs my children will someday encounter are the potential scenarios they might place themselves in. If they share my love of vice, particularly under-age drinking, we all have cause to worry.

The first place I ever traveled to for an extended period of time, meaning more than two weeks, was Russia. I studied there for a semester in both high school and college. I was fifteen when I arrived in Moscow the first time, where I gleaned a multitude of cultural highlights, from the Bolshoi Theater to traditional, Eastern European depression. My main focus of study was Vodka 101.

Back on US soil at the age of sixteen, I was listing all of my newfound life skills on my résumé and discovered that in addition to championship status at consuming vodka and cigarettes, I was also a master of the Russian accent. At this time in my life, I had no problem lying with every other word, which is what being sixteen is all about.

My seventeen-year-old stepbrother and I developed a plan. We drove through Caroline County, Virginia, to towns not big enough to make the map. He waited in the car. I went into the liquor store alone.

The clerk always started: "Can I help you?"

My response: "Uh . . . *Govaritye li vuey pah russkie?* Do you speak Russian?"

"No, I don't speak Russian."

"I yam looking for . . . do you have . . . vodka? I want buy vodka but I yam student at university from Russia. Dey don't giff me, how you say, de license, because I cannot rread de signs?" My *R*s were rolled and exaggerated, and I pronounced every *H* as if clearing my throat.

A little over a year had passed since the dissolution of *CCCP*, so the responses, in a dozen liquor stores, were similar.

"I've never met a Russian."

"All the way from Russia."

"Welcome to America!"

They were pure kindness with minimal skepticism. You'd think that in a backwoods Virginia liquor store, I might have encountered some hostility, but I never did. It was a few rich kids from my high school farther north who called me "Commie" and looked upon my study of Russian with disdain. I find it difficult to take seriously anyone who uses "Commie" as an insult. It's a sure sign of being stuck in the eighties, like shoulder pads and aviator jackets.

The Virginia clerks never asked for a passport or student ID, or wondered how I'd arrived at their den of intriguing liquids without a license. If I sensed reluctance, I just threw in straight Russian. "I'm frrom *Moskovskaya Oblast*, de Moscow rregion." Or I'd mutter to myself, as if trying to translate in my head, "*Idti na xhouyu e youb tvoyou mat.*" It didn't matter that I'd said, "Go fuck yourself and then fuck your mother." It was authentic and guttural and turned them blind to everything else about me that screamed TEENAGER.

When I had them, I'd push it further. "And, do have, do you have, how is called . . . malt liquor?" This was for my waiting stepbrother, who hadn't yet accepted vodka as his personal savior, as I had. One guy threw in my cigarettes for free. He was flannel, country, and kind, the type I would have judged, had I not wanted so much from him. That particular clerk insisted on carrying my brown bag of vices out to my car, where he locked eyes with my stepbrother, detecting deception. I stared at my stepbrother, willing him not to speak and somehow generate a Slavic aura. If only those cheekbones had a more Motherland slant.

"Tank you so much, is verry good, verry happy."

"All right, then," he said, realizing he had been duped.

As we drove away, guilt grew from my dishonesty, but I had means enough to drink it away.

Nora and I also did our fair share of drinking together. At seventeen, we drove to Ocean City, Maryland, for an off-season weekend at the beach. We checked into a scuzzy hotel, had a few mixed drinks, and then went to walk the boardwalk. As we walked along, we saw two men coming toward us. They were in their thirties and not unattractive. As they passed us, one of the men said to Nora, "Hey, you want a piece of pizza?"

"Heck yeah," Nora said.

Before we knew it, we were sitting at a greasy pizza joint with these two older guys. I was bothered by them, nagged by the thought they were being deceptive. One of them had a dog tag–type chain around his neck that disappeared under his shirt.

"What's at the end of your chain, there?" I asked, knowing the answer.

"Oh." He smiled. "Those are my dog tags. They're very personal; I don't show them to anyone."

Nora began talking about how old we were and how much alcohol we'd consumed, oblivious to the kicks I delivered to her under the table.

"I really want to see those dog tags," I interrupted.

His name was Dave, and he relented and pulled out his badge.

"I knew it!" I said.

Nora's jaw dropped. The cops then proceeded to tell us how they weren't on duty, didn't want to bust anyone, and were just out having a good time. This did not put me at ease, but I was seventeen and therefore invincible.

We ended up going to their vacation house, which they'd

rented with half a dozen other cops. We played cards and drinking games, though this was one of the few instances in my life when I stopped drinking from fear of the situation. Part of my apprehension was from the age difference. Just like Skankella and Pigstopher, I was troubled by the fact that these men in their thirties wanted to party with teenagers. Another danger sign was the storytelling. A recent prison riot was big in the news at the time, and they bragged about how many inmates they'd shot or beaten while regaining control of the situation. I grew more fearful as the evening wore on and insisted we leave before there was any breaching of panties, forcible or otherwise.

Officers Dave and Randy drove us back to our hotel in their police cruiser, drunk themselves, at ninety miles per hour with sirens blaring at two o'clock in the morning.

I'm not going to lock my girls away in a tower, but memories like this scare the hell out of me. As a result, I'm determined to teach them to be kind and open minded but also coldhearted and suspicious.

There are other wisdoms I'd like to impart on my children that have less to do with actual physical danger. For instance, a lesson in amateur stripping. I admit to having once taken to the stage. I didn't bare all, as I was plagued at the time by a large pimple on my buttock. I did, however, learn a few things that come in handy for anyone who decides to approach the pole.

First: If your balance is severely compromised, do not attempt to twirl around the pole. You will fall and injure your body almost as much as your ego. When you twirl around the pole for the first time, you're not prepared for the momentum and speed. Depending on how much alcohol you've consumed, the results can be disastrous.

Second: Try to think back to when you dressed yourself. During my little dance, though I didn't bare all, I did lift my skirt during the finale to show my undies. What I'd forgotten, through the course of an alcoholic evening, was that I'd selected my most comfortable pair of underwear, which are solid white and also happen to be the largest pair of panties ever made. The amount of fabric used in making this garment could clothe a small tribe. As a result, my grand finale was more comedic than sexy, but hey, I earned a whopping two dollars for my dance. Both bills were pity payments from the professional dancers, but I'm not about to bite the hand that feeds.

* * *

CHAPTER 10

Mamas, Don't Let Your Babies Grow Up to Be Serial Killers

O f all the things that parents hope to shield their children from, I'm less concerned about the usual suspects of drugs, sex, and violence, and more worried about the evils of chewing gum. Okay, I'm trying to shield *myself* from chewing gum. And I know it's not *evil*, but it still scares me.

I am gum-phobic. There is an official word for this. Not because that's logical, but because uncommon phobias always have words for them, when you wouldn't think a word would be necessary. For instance, if a person has a fear of the color yellow, can't we just call them yellow-phobic? What's wrong with a little off-the-cuff hyphenating here and there? But there *is* an official word for the fear of yellow, xanthophobia.

There are four words just for the fear of hair: chaetophobia, trichopathophobia, trichophobia, and hypertrichophobia. I'm not hair-phobic like I'm gum-phobic, but I do agree that hair is horrifying. It's okay when still attached to a head, but the second a strand is free of its scalp, it acquires amazing powers to navigate its way into food or cleavage or butt crack. When I find such hairs gone wild, all I can do is pray that they were once my own. Why has no one made a horror movie about a clump of hair coming to life from a shower drain and terrorizing a small New England town?

The fear of chewing gum is chiclephobia, begging the question: Which came first, the Chiclet or the chiclephobic? And chiclephobic I am. I find it disturbing to masticate without eventually consuming what you are chewing. I hate it when people are working, no matter what their profession, and chewing gum. And I despise those who take their gum out of the mouth but save it for later use. Is gum really that expensive?

I fear stepping in gum, as do most people. I'm terrified by the idea of touching what someone else has molested with their tongue. If you must chew gum, you are socially obligated to dispose of it by first wadding it safely into the midst of a very large paper towel, tissue, or piece of paper. Using a little corner of a napkin is not acceptable. The gum must be rendered incapable of sticking to anything else for the rest of time.

People who allow their children to chew gum in other people's homes are treasonous. And if, in my home, a parent says something to their child along the lines of, "Now, make sure you put that in the trash when you're done," they're basically telling me that I'll be spending the following afternoon cleaning gum off of my carpet, which is my own personal hell. Along the same lines, don't bring your dog to my house if it's going to shit in my living room.

Gum doesn't just scare me when it's past its prime. I also have a severe aversion to gum as it is being chewed. A friend of mine manages to clench his gum in between his teeth on one side while still forming intelligible words with the rest of his mouth. A talent, yes, but the gum is visible to me as he does this. I never really hear anything he says. I'm pretty sure he thinks I'm slow. My phobia turns me into a moron. Rather than deal with my issues, I've simply instituted a no-gum rule when it comes to my children. I speak of gum as most parents speak of heroin.

Not all of my rules are as illogical as the gum rule. I'm big on hand-washing and am distressed by the number of people who fail to wash their hands after using the bathroom. Every other week at Mike's office, I'd don my janitorial cap and clean both the men's and women's restrooms. I thought of myself as janitor, while Mike associates any woman cleaning with a cheap, French-maid Halloween costume. He views wielding a feather duster as a seduction attempt, despite the fact that I could be clad in sweats at the time. He once approached me playfully with a feather duster, implying some sort of flirtation.

"Unless you're turned on by dust mites and bacteria," I said, "get that thing away from me."

The restrooms at work were put to use by two small businesses, and the collective users represented an equal number of men and women. In the course of my cleaning, one of my tasks was to refill the soap dispensers, yet I rarely found a need to do so in the men's restroom. The soap did not get used, leading me to the conclusion that men must view their penises as inherently pristine. Mike confessed to harboring this belief.

"You don't ever wash your hands, do you?" I asked.

"My hands are clean," he said.

"But you're supposed to wash your hands after going to the

bathroom."

"They don't get dirty."

"You open the door."

"With my elbows."

"You flush the toilet."

"With my foot."

"You touch your penis."

"Which is clean."

"You think your penis has some sort of built-in, self-cleaning mechanism?"

"Yes. Yes, it does."

His theory is that if he were to wash his hands, he would touch the sink and the soap dispenser, which contain more bacteria than they help to eradicate.

Maybe it's a phobia. Mike washes his hands only after engaging in a construction project involving paint, tar, caulk, or dangerous chemicals. I think he gets it from his father. My father-in-law can function entirely oblivious to the fact that his hands are covered in cocktail sauce or his famous balslamic marianade. Before you know it, these substances have been relayed to every remote control, door handle, and light switch in his path. I creep along behind him with a pack of baby wipes in a feeble attempt to control the spread of crusting condiments throughout my house.

After a visit from my father-in-law, I once found myself in our kitchen, stalking a fly on the wall. I crept silently up to the little beast, rolled-up magazine in hand. And then I stopped, because he had that look about him that flies get, that *challenge*. "I'm taking off as soon as you move," the fly said. "Think you can get me? Do you?"

Whack!

"Got him!" I said.

"Yeah, honey," my husband said, "you got the pork."

"What?"

"That was pork on the wall."

I surveyed the damage only to find that I had just smeared a fly-sized glob of barbequed pork along the white wall of our kitchen. My eyesight is not stellar.

"Why is there pork on the wall?!"

"I don't know," Mike answered. "My dad was here."

Because a fear of hand-washing has proven to infiltrate multiple generations of my husband's side of the family, I'm determined to instill the importance of it into my children.

With hand-washing, I'm usually on the same page as other parents. When my daughters see other parents giving their children gum, though, I am automatically the bad guy. But I treat it like others treat religion; it is a basic principle of our family. As in, We Don't Chew Gum, just like Catholics Don't Eat Meat on Fridays During Lent. When they're older, I'm sure they'll throw my hypocrisy back at me. "How come I'm not allowed to chew gum, but you're allowed to drink two bottles of wine?" I'll simply inform them that alcohol kills germs while gum spreads them.

The best way to approach things like this probably involves instilling in my children a terrifying, albeit completely false belief. Something along the lines of: Gum will cause a mutant alien baby to begin growing inside you. Or maybe: Every time you chew gum, a unicorn dies a painful and horrible death. No one wants to lie to their kids, but sometimes it can't be helped.

* * *

A less competent liar than me does not exist. It is a talent I lost once I hit adulthood. I simply refuse to lie, not out of altruism, but from fear of the embarrassment of getting caught. I'd rather eat a live worm.

In the third grade, I had a sprained ankle. One of the best injury accessories to show off at school is a cast. The instant popularity that results from students wanting to sign it is as close to intoxication as a small child should get. Crutches are the runner-up to the coveted cast, and in the third grade, I was lucky enough to get crutches. My fame would not be short-lived; I would cling to it dearly.

"Are you okay?" kids asked.

"What happened?"

"Does it hurt?"

"Can I try your crutches?"

"Are you going to live?"

"Well," I responded, "the doctor said it's just too soon to tell."

After a day on crutches, my armpits ached, and the bruising on my shins from my clumsy handling of them hurt worse than my injured ankle. But I kept the permanent grimace of pain firmly plastered on my face for two solid weeks.

Emilia's shown similar inclinations. She'd often tell me that she needed a Band-Aid for an owie and then point to the affliction, which was actually a freckle or something she'd drawn on her skin with marker. She also practiced her cough a lot and prefaced it with, "Listen to this, Mama. I'm really sick."

During the third week of my half-fabricated injured ankle, I sat at my desk when Mrs. Mallard, who was a snarky sort, called out the name of my reading group. I can't remember what the name was, but we were the smart, unattractive kids. "Word Nerds" will suffice.

"Word Nerds! Word Nerds!" Mrs. Mallard announced.

When a reading group was called, all of those students would scramble to a small U-shaped table, each vying for a choice position right up front, because that's what nerds do. For some reason, on that day, I forgot about my injury, my reliable means of gaining sympathy and pity. I moved like a cheetah struck by lightning, barely able to blink in the time I shot up from my seat and muscled my way into a spot at the table. We Word Nerds sat, silent and well-behaved, waiting for Mrs. Mallard to begin the lesson.

She stared at me, reveling in the silence.

"Well," she said, with a dramatic pause to be sure the entire classroom was listening, "I guess you're feeling better then, aren't you?"

My wide eyes looked up at her expectant smirk. "Yes," I whispered.

The crutches retired, and I cried that night. Not over the end of my glorious fifteen minutes, but at the spotlight Mrs. Mallard placed on me, a liar exposed for all the class to see.

Lying is something that most parents find common ground on. My husband and I both want our children to be honest, but we also recognize that bending the truth and testing boundaries are a part of growing up. When one of our daughters is caught in a lie, we are likely to respond in similar ways, hopefully with a little understanding of what it was once like to be a kid.

There are other aspects of life that fall strictly to one parent or the other. Like hand-washing, I want to make sure my children learn *my* take when it comes to dinner table etiquette. My mother was big on this, though I cannot recall an instance of actually eating at a dinner table. We ate in various shifts in front of the television. We ate while reading, working, or doing homework. We ate hunched over the sink for easy cleanup. But I still somehow reached adulthood with a clear sense of dinner table etiquette. These rules were absent in my husband's upbringing. There are plenty of other areas where my husband is welcome to have full reign, but I claim supreme authority in the area of food.

When in the presence of food, Mike experiences a fierce rush of survival instinct, which commands him to hoard food before the rest of the family swoops in and leaves him hungry. Perhaps this stems from being the youngest of three. This should no longer be an issue; I cook for legions and spend a fair amount of each day making sure that my husband does not go hungry. But I can still see the panic in his eyes.

He's been known to walk by our daughters while they eat and swipe one of their crackers, which is creating in them the same irrational fear regarding there not being enough food. I'm trying to break the cycle before it bleeds into future generations.

The only time Mike loses his appetite is when he is sick. I've never understood this, the concept of not wanting food when ill. Eating to me is the ultimate comfort, and I am convinced that I could eat my way through any number of infectious diseases or tragedies.

Mike is not immune to the differences in our upbringing, and he's agreed that the etiquette issue is all mine. (Conversely, I have agreed never to try to teach our children to dance. Mike's side of the family is gifted with incredible dancing genes. I just have mom jeans.)

The problem with etiquette is that when someone who is not your own child violates the rules of etiquette, you cannot tell them, because that would violate the rules of etiquette. You have to lie and pretend you aren't appalled, and lying violates the rules of etiquette. All this violating makes me feel awfully dirty.

Mealtime etiquette is easy. Along with the basics of guests first, ladies first, and try to use your napkin, there are a few others worth mentioning:

1. Do not allow stray bits of food to hang out on your chin throughout a meal. Isn't that bothersome, anyway? How can one not feel a big glob of marinara adhering itself to one's face? It's not like dirt on your shoe. It's on your *face*.

2. Shut your mouth when chewing your food. I realize that we all think we're eating quietly, but it's worth it to turn off the television and listen so that you can fully realize the audible horrors coming from your mouth. And for the love of all things culinary, don't talk and eat at the same time.

3. Use your knife, not your finger, to push food onto your fork. It's not there just to stab an intruder who might show up during mealtime. Seriously. It has many other uses.

4. A forkful of food is only the amount of food that fits on a fork. If a long, buttery green bean or dangling tentacle of pasta is hanging down, don't try to shove it in your mouth anyway or slurp up the rest. No one wants to see that.

5. During the course of a meal, make eye contact with

others. If you're not going to engage with others at the table, you might as well go eat while hunched over the sink. Cleanup is way easier.

6. When serving yourself, always be conscious of how many people have yet to eat and how much food is left. Remember learning fractions in elementary school? This is what those lessons were all about, teaching us not to be dicks at the dinner table.

7. As an adult, if you are going to fight over the bill, then *really* fight for it. If all you've got is a half-hearted "No, really, I can't let you," as you feign a reach for your wallet, then you're better off just saying, "Thank you."

8. Share. Always offer someone else the bigger portion, the last of something. And offer genuinely; "Are you going to eat that?" doesn't count. "Are you going to eat that?" is passive-aggressive, and you want to save your passive-aggressiveness for the *after*-dinner family gathering.

Unless you are starving, and I mean really physically starving, as in skin, bones, distended belly, and circling vultures, then being hungry is not a valid excuse for ignoring any of the rules of mealtime etiquette.

Basically, I have the household rules all figured out: No gum, wash your hands, try not to lie too much, and don't be an ass at the dinner table. If we had boys, I would also include: Don't be a serial killer. I'm all about encouraging children to follow their dreams and to let them know that they can be whatever they want to be. Except for serial killers. We only have girls, so I'm confident this isn't something I'll have to address.

* * *

CHAPTER 11

Mother of the Year

Whenever I start to unfavorably judge myself as a mother, which, truth be told, really doesn't happen all that often, I stop and think of my own mother, who is far from perfect but did a wonderful job just the same, and hope that my children will view me in a similar light. My mother excels at highlighting her own failures. Her self-deprecation and the occasional snort in her laughter make up for all of her deficiencies in punctuality and the culinary arts.

"I'm no Mother of the Year," she'd say, picking me up late from soccer practice.

"Sorry, I'm no June Cleaver," as I'd hop out of the car in the morning and run the last quarter mile to school while she accepted a speeding ticket.

"Martha Stewart, I am not," while serving up her famous black-bottom bread or a steaming bowl of ramen.

She also never demanded recognition for the good, even when she deserved it. Finding time to take me to Baker Park to feed the fat and hostile ducks could not have been easy as a divorced mother of two. She constantly battled exhaustion, along with the dishes, laundry, job, and temperaments of stubborn children. She never bitched about such things, or whined about her own tumultuous childhood.

As an adult, now juggling it all myself, I will forever appreciate the fact that my mother gets me. In each other's company, we laugh until one of us urinates involuntarily, which may not sound like positive mother-daughter bonding, but it is. Our relationship thrives on humor, but we also share a touching fascination with morbidity.

"Merry Christmas, Mom!"

"Merry Christmas! Did you get my package?"

"Yes! Thank you for the books! I'm especially excited about *Dark Dreams: Sexual Violence, Homicide, and the Criminal Mind.*"

"I know, that one looks really good," she agreed. "I was hoping maybe you'll let me read it when you're done."

"Of course. I've got a John Douglas book for you, too." At this, my mom let out a shriek of delight, the sound most women her age make only when learning of an impending and welcome grandbaby, because that's just how we feel about legendary criminal profilers.

When I became a parent, my mother was my greatest reassurance in terms of battling all of the crap that people shove down your throat as far as what you should and should not do. Her all-purpose advice was "Don't listen to them; do whatever works."

Parents who "cosleep" with their children look down upon those who put their babies in their own rooms, labeling them uncaring and selfish. The uncaring parents equally judge the cosleepers as overparenting.

Emilia slept in our room for nine months in a cosleeper, basically a crib that butted up against the side of our bed (my side, of course). As soon as we moved her into her own room, she graciously began sleeping through the night and we wished we'd made the move sooner. With Ivy, we were determined not to make the same mistake and moved her into her own room as soon as possible. But all children are different, and we didn't yet know that Ivy would refuse sleep in any room, under any circumstances.

Periodically, I encountered whack-job mothers who were shocked by the fact that I moved an infant to a separate room to sleep at night. Mommy and Me classes are fertile ground for whack-jobs.

"Studies show that cosleeping with your children provides them with greater self-esteem," one woman said. "That contact with your baby is *so* important."

"I have plenty of contact with my baby," I reasoned. "It's not like I keep her in the closet with crackers and a dish of water."

"But you've placed her in another room to sleep?"

"She sleeps in *her* room. You're making it sound like I throw her on a dog bed in the basement."

"And why have you chosen this arrangement?"

"I think it's important for them to be able to sleep on their own."

"And does she sleep well in there all by herself?"

"Well, not exactly," I admitted.

"That intimacy is really important for the relationship between mother and baby."

"So, you still sleep with your kids?" I asked.

"Oh, yes!" she said.

"And how's your sex life?"

"Excuse me?"

"How's your marriage?"

"What?"

"Get it *on* much?"

"That's not your business."

"That's a 'no' if I've ever heard one. I'd think that having a baby in your bed puts a bit of a damper on the flame, if you know what I mean."

"What happens in my bedroom is private."

"Apparently not. The way you describe it, it sounds pretty crowded in there."

She moved on to someone else.

The issue of breastfeeding was worse. I understand that the big bad formula companies brainwashed women into believing that their breast milk wasn't good enough, but that's long since been righted, and the pressure we now have to breastfeed is overwhelming. Mothers are in essence told that if they selfishly choose not to breastfeed their children, those children will be sick and stupid as a result. I have my faults, but I was raised on formula and can firmly assert that I am neither sick nor stupid.

I could handle the toe-curling pain of a baby latching on, and I dealt with the aching, leaking boobs and their accompanying unattractive bras and breast pads. I even begrudgingly accepted the fact that despite having made it through pregnancy, I *still* had to alter my alcohol consumption. I could not, however, handle mastitis.

We visited my in-laws, who were house sitting on an island in southeast Alaska where Mike grew up. My husband and mother-in-law ran errands in town, and I remained on the island with infant Emilia and my father-in-law, who puttered about the property. It was time to feed, and my breasts had been bothering me more than usual. I unbound the boulders to find red streaks covering my chest. Breastfeeding brought tears to my eyes. My breasts were infected, I was trapped on an island in Alaska with my baby, and the only adult to turn to was my father-in-law. He is a wonderful man, but the last person you want to have to discuss a breast ailment with is your father-in-law. I would rather chat about a yeast infection with the pope.

Later that day, I was treated at the clinic of the Sitka hospital. Sitka is a small town, where everyone knows everyone else, so checking into the clinic meant meeting Mike's high school classmates, former babysitters, childhood neighbors, and old flames.

"Oh, you're Mike Turner's wife! It's so nice to meet you!"

"Thanks, it's nice to meet you, too."

"What are you doing here? Is everything okay?"

"Oh, yes," I assured them. "I have an . . . infection." This did not sound good, and I hastened to add, "in my *breast*," as if that made it better.

Why didn't I just lie? I could have said I was there to be seen for allergies or that I'd pulled a muscle in my back. Better yet, why hadn't I just blamed the baby? Babies are constantly going to the doctor for various suspected ailments or abnormal secretions, so no one would have thought a thing about it. I know that I wasn't on the tip of the town's tongue, but it felt like the daily newspaper was headlining the story. "Mike Turner Returns to Sitka with Wife and Her Infected Breasts."

A family friend called into town from his fishing vessel at sea to inquire if I was okay. While this was genuine concern for my well-being, I did not like having my breasts bob up regularly in conversation.

Most women manage to avoid infection and have a healthy attitude toward breastfeeding. It may not be their favorite activity, but they appreciate the fact that they can provide the best possible nutritional start for their child. Some women enjoy breastfeeding and find it difficult to give up. Then there are the clichéd characters who breastfeed way too long, when their children have long since learned to walk and talk and unbutton Mommy's blouse.

And then there are those who *really* love it. As in, they still talk about how much they enjoyed breastfeeding their children, despite the fact that their children are now entering the labor pool. This may be accompanied by an unhealthy attachment to their breast milk. A friend of mine keeps a frozen sample of her breast milk in her freezer. She is in her sixties, her children are pushing forty, and I can see no possible reason for this other than for purposes of scientific research, in which case it should be in a lab. It's downright creepy; I don't want to encounter forty-year-old frozen breast milk while searching for the chilled vodka.

* * *

The issues that parents wrestle with in the beginning, such as birthing techniques, sleeping arrangements, and feeding habits, don't concern me anymore. There are choices there that are neither right nor wrong and not worth my time.

I'm also unperturbed by the looks from others when I walk into the liquor store with a baby on my hip or a car seat in tow. I typically try to go to the liquor store when my children are not with me, but sometimes it can't be helped. It's not like I'm buying alcohol to give to my child. It's not as if Mommy passes out on the couch in the evenings or forgets that her children are in the bathtub. Just like babies need their binkies, sometimes mommies and daddies need their toddies.

What do concern me in terms of appropriate parenting are my heat-of-the-moment behaviors, the ones that I don't hide away from my children, like road rage.

I was driving along, my daughters buckled snugly in the back, when I noticed a tailgater.

"Aagghh!" I jumped in my seat, a reaction appropriate to discovering a wart on one's buttock. A wart with long hairs. You wonder how long it's been there and whether or not it poses a danger to your health.

The driver behind me appeared set on hovering as close as possible to my bumper without actually rear-ending me. Sort of like an obnoxious sibling who holds their finger an inch from your face while chanting, "I'm not touching you, I'm not touching you," until you reach the point of annoyance where you suddenly try to bite their finger off to put the matter to rest.

Tailgaters are ubiquitous, and usually I can ignore them, but this particular driver took vehicular hostilities to a new level. I brought my moderate pace down to a crawl. The wart turned on his brights. There's nothing like bright lights in broad daylight to take me down an RPM. I continued puttering. It's not that I refuse to engage, but I prefer the passive-aggressive approach.

Was this an example of why people put "Baby on Board" stickers on their cars? And does that really work? It seems to me that an asshole is going to remain so whether or not you have offspring in your vehicle. Or are the "Baby on Board" stickers there as an excuse for overly cautious driving? As in, "Please don't hate me for driving so slow, it's just that I have a baby in the car and I'm *freaking out!*" If that's the motivation, then we should have similar stickers for the elderly. It could read "Old People Driving," as a way of saying, "Don't rush me, jackass. One more fender-bender and they take my keys away, so I have to be really fucking careful."

When given the opportunity, the tailgating wart zoomed past me. It was time for that awkward moment when you finally see your foe, make your gestures, mouth your insults. I slammed my hand against the window for emphasis as I gave him the finger. My wedding ring clanked hard on the glass. At the same time, I yelled "Fuck you!" with a good deal of volume. The expletive had been welling up inside me for five blocks. Wart had driven by me so fast, he probably didn't even see my hand gesture, and he certainly wouldn't have been able to hear what I yelled. But my daughters saw and heard. Immediately I felt like an ass. A warty ass.

I couldn't let it go, all day long, my idiocy at having been suckered in and therefore no better than the tailgater. My anger ate at me, and guilt over my reaction in front of my daughters tormented me. I wallowed in the underlying fear that this scene would repeat itself every morning, this encounter with the wart that must live in the same neighborhood, and with whom I apparently share at least a partial commute. An irrational but thoroughly convincing part of my mind suggested that we should probably move.

When road rage is over, when the bad guy has taken a different exit, I breathe a sigh of relief. The concern, that I have angered someone to the point where they are going to follow me to my destination and shoot me, dissipates. That's my second greatest fear behind the wheel. The number-one fear, of course, is that I will injure a child, that an innocent but wayward little tot on a tricycle will ride into the path of my approaching vehicle. This should top everyone's list, as far as vehicular fears go.

It's always a relief when the confrontation has passed and I can drift back into the anonymity of traffic. But my husband is in real estate and has branded our car, which creates the new fear that this person will find me after the fact via the enormous website stenciled across my rear window, and *then* shoot me. Or worse, they'll go to the website, see my husband's picture, assume he was the driver, and hunt him down and shoot *him*. I probably just shouldn't drive.

Worse than looking in the rearview mirror to discover a tailgater on your ass is noticing that your child appears to be leaning over at an odd angle in the backseat. You stop the car and examine the situation to find that while you did place your child in the car seat, you failed to buckle them in, a complicated process involving a twelve-point harness and safety system.

I've asked my mom and others of her generation what they did with us before car seats.

"I just threw you in the back, and you flew all over the place," my mother informed me.

"Did we ever get hurt?" I asked.

"Nope, you just sort of bounced off of things. Babies are very resilient that way."

"Did you put seatbelts on us?"

"Seatbelts? We didn't have seatbelts."

"Well, what about when we were newborns? You didn't just throw us in the backseat then, did you?"

"Of course not," she said. "I put you in a shoebox on the floor of the passenger seat."

When I'd forget to buckle my children, which I believe all parents do on occasion, whether or not they admit to it, I'd just try to right the situation without muttering "Bad mom, bad mom," to myself. My daughters liked to repeat everything they heard, and inevitably we'd arrive at day care with Emilia announcing to her class that she was not buckled in her seat during the car ride, and Ivy singing "Bad mom, bad mom" to the tune of *Twinkle, Twinkle, Little Star*.

* * *

CHAPTER 12

Dinosaur Chickens

I would like to require people to wear T-shirts or name tags that warn others what type of person they are. We could start with categories like Asshole, Elitist, Fetishist, and Martyr. It could revolutionize the dating scene. Self-Centered Prick and Codependent Whiner could learn important aspects of each other ahead of time and decide if they still want to give it a go. I hope that we can institute some sort of policy like this before my daughters reach the dating age.

Until I can turn that into law, I will continue to use the salad method. You can tell a lot about a person by inviting them over for dinner and asking them to bring a salad. There are people who make a salad with nothing more than spinach and sliced tomatoes. I *like* spinach and sliced tomatoes, there's nothing *wrong* with spinach and sliced tomatoes, but this is a salad without pizzazz, if it even counts as a salad. You could argue that it's just two items and doesn't deserve to be called a dish. When it comes to a salad, you should at least have enough items that listing them necessitates a comma. Spinach and tomatoes doesn't cut it.

Then there are the guests who suffer from lachanophobia, commonly known as the fear of vegetables.

Lachanophobe: "What can we bring tomorrow?"

Me: "How about a salad?"

Lachanophobe: "Like potato salad?"

Me: "I was thinking more like a traditional salad."

Lachanophobe: "Oh, like macaroni salad?"

Me: "Maybe a salad with vegetables in it."

Lachanophobe: "Coleslaw?"

Me: "No. A salad. Nothing with mayonnaise. Must contain lettuce."

Lachanophobe: "Oh, right. A salad."

She showed up with a bag of shredded lettuce and a bottle of ranch.

If your guests bring a salad that features crushed Doritos, Fritos, or Ritz crackers, then I hope you didn't go to any great lengths with the main course beyond that of macaroni and cheese with Spam, or hot dog and tater tot casserole. Put away the Malbec and break out the Pabst Blue Ribbon.

Mike and I were once served tater tot casserole at a dinner party. We arrived, bottle of wine in hand, to find that dinner was a combination of Ore-Ida Tots, cream of mushroom soup, and cheese. My abdominal distress was considerable. Had we left a minute later, I might have shat myself.

Then there's the other end of the buffet, the guests who bring a salad with roasted pine nuts, hearts of palm, jicama, homemade sourdough croutons, and a red wine, raspberry, and fennel vinaigrette, which probably doesn't taste very good, but you ooh and ahh over it politely because it's pretty. These people make you wish you'd prepared risotto instead of chili.

I'd like to start asking people what kind of salad they eat before I have any interaction with them. I could save myself a lot of heartache and indigestion.

Food is such a good indicator of character that I'd try to peer into the lunch boxes at my children's day care to see what the other parents were feeding their kids. I wanted this information before agreeing to a play date or birthday party.

I know that kids are finicky, but that doesn't mean it's okay to keep them on a diet of Kool-Aid, Cheetos, and chocolate pudding. And what's with the two-year-olds delivered to day care in the mornings with their sixteen-ounce Starbucks Frappuccinos, complete with whipped cream? I can't decide whether I'm more disturbed by the sugar content, the cost, or the fact that the newest Starbucks addict is still in diapers. On top of all that, you now have a classroom of children crying because they don't get a drive-thru dessert masked as coffee at 7 a.m., too. And which is worse, I wonder, giving your toddler a dessert at 7 a.m., or coffee?

I didn't feed my kids tofu and brown rice, and I never made them homemade organic baby food. I strove for that happy medium, but it was a happy medium that occasionally included a Happy Meal.

For three years, I included vegetables with Emilia's lunch, whether at day care or at home. For three years, I threw those vegetables away or ate them myself. Then one day, she started chomping on a carrot. I praised her so much that she began picking up carrots and screaming, "Mama! Look what I'm about to do!" She'd slowly tease out a bite of the carrot, and I had to oblige with a reaction akin to winning the lottery.

"That's great, Emilia!" I'd jump up and down. We'd high-five.

When she first began feeding herself, Emilia would eat with such enthusiasm that she would cram entire bananas into her mouth, or whole hot dogs. She would put more food into her mouth at one time than could possibly fit, and then use her palm to shove the food in if it threatened to emerge.

We went to Casanova's, our favorite pizza joint, with Uncle Virgil, next to whom Emilia insisted on sitting. This restaurant was the lone consistent establishment we'd frequented since having children. It was casual enough for kids, but still had elegance and charm so that we didn't feel like we were eating at Chuck E. Cheese, which is Mike's personal version of hell. In the winter, the floor of Casanova's would be home to space heaters that glowed a menacing orange and beckoned for small fingers to touch them. We didn't mind, though. This kept families with more obnoxious and unruly children from dining there, and at worst, we figured our kids would learn the hard way not to touch heating coils.

All was well with our group until the pizza came and Emilia began demonstrating her talent of cramming an obscene amount of food in her mouth.

"Holy mother of shitballs!" Virgil cried.

"Virgil!" I hissed. "I will not allow you to be around my child if you speak like that!"

"I'm sorry, but do you not see what's going on here?"

"What?" I asked.

"Emilia! She's going to choke. Somebody *do* something!"

"She's not choking," Mike assured his brother. "She's just . . .

hungry."

"I'm sorry," he said again, "but I'm the most inappropriate, unhealthy person I know, and *that*"—he pointed to Emilia—"is inappropriate and unhealthy."

When Virgil identifies something as inappropriate and unhealthy, it's a good indication that we should pay attention. Emilia thankfully grew out of this approach to food. While the speed with which she ate slowed to a normal pace, her excitement was undiminished.

My nieces were over for a play date, and Sandi dropped them off with snacks. This was good, as my nieces are older than my girls and were at the age of furious growth that demanded they eat every four minutes or turn to dust. One of the snacks they brought was a package of peanut butter crackers, the kind that have existed since the beginning of time. A peanut butter–like substance is sandwiched between two crackers the color of traffic cones. A lone cracker remained at the end of their visit, and I included this with Emilia's dinner. When she saw her plate, she gasped.

"Mama! What did you make?" She gestured to the cracker as if it was pure, edible happiness.

"Uh. I made a . . . cracker," I said.

"Mama!" she gasped again. "I *love* this cracker."

"I'm glad," I said. "It took me a long time to . . . make."

* * *

One of my greatest pet peeves before becoming a parent was the family that goes to a restaurant and somehow turns a blind eye to their children as they smear mustard against the wall, fling spaghetti to the floor, and burst the eardrums of other patrons with their screaming. I vowed never to become that parent. As a result, we were careful when we took our children out to eat. The conditions had to be just right, with sufficient napping and temperaments in place before we attempted to dine among strangers.

Babies are fun to take to restaurants. Preschoolers are usually all right. But there's a deadly age of misbehavior in between that the general public should be shielded from at all cost. It's the age when tempers flare but before the child can effectively communicate, so they shriek and hurl utensils instead. This is one of the few instances in which problems will not be solved by consuming more alcohol, at least not until you get home. We could usually tell within the first five minutes of sitting down at a restaurant if we were going to make it through the meal. If the answer was no, we'd leave and resign ourselves to dinosaur-shaped chicken nuggets (known in our house as "dinosaur chickens"), Goldfish crackers, and entertainment by Pixar. This shouldn't be taken as defeat, as it's a far better course of action than trying to suffer through.

The other problem comes at the end, when for some reason, as your children begin to melt like microwaved Velveeta, it becomes impossible to get the check. Until you stand up and start walking toward the door. Then the check appears rather quickly.

When my daughters were in these difficult stages, I'd occasionally attempt in vain to have a real meal at the dinner table without the accompaniment of television. And by "real" meal, I mean that all four family members sat down at the same table, at the same time. Inevitably, I'd spend forty-five minutes preparing a feast that I did not get to eat and another forty-five scraping congealed ketchup off the floor. It was a tiresome and thankless routine that I never managed to sustain for more than a few days.

Mike had no expectations of adult food prepared at the end of *every* day. "Did you cook tonight or are we drinking for dinner?" he'd ask. I'd raise my wineglass in silent response.

While the adults learned to forgo solids, Ivy demanded meals at all hours of the day and night.

"More more breakfast," she'd insist at nine o'clock at night.

"It's not time to eat right now," I'd tell her.

"Dinner?"

"No, we just had dinner."

"More more dinner?"

"No, it's bedtime."

"Yunch?"

"Sleep."

"Snack?"

"Sleep."

"Goldfish?"

"Night-night."

"Waffles?"

* * *

We drove along Idaho's I-84 at the start of a family vacation when I noticed an attractive, twenty-something male in the car next to ours, trying to get my attention.

"Check it out, Mike. This guy is really flirting with me," I said. Mike glanced over.

"Are you sure he's flirting with you?" he asked.

"Yes, I'm sure. He just pointed to me and said something like 'You're hot.'" I winked back at the guy, who was doing his best to match our speed in a silver sports car, a vehicle that had obviously never hosted the likes of car seats or Cheerios trapped for eternity in every crevice.

"That seems odd," Mike said.

"Why is that odd? You don't think guys flirt with me? You'd be *pissed* if you knew how many guys flirt with me. I get hit on *all* the time."

"I'm not saying guys don't flirt with you, I'm saying it's unlikely that this particular guy is flirting with you at this particular moment."

"What, you think he's too good-looking for me? Too young? Be honest. What is it?" I demanded.

"It's not that. It just seems odd that he'd flirt with a woman who's obviously in a car with her husband and two kids on a family vacation. I mean, we're towing a utility trailer with a portable crib and a high chair in it. That doesn't exactly scream 'available.'"

"Oh stop," I said. "You're just jealous." He had a point, though, and I glanced behind us just in time to see the high chair fly out of our utility trailer into the path of the unfortunate vehicles trapped in our wake.

"Shit! What was that?" Mike said, nervously watching the rearview mirror.

"Uh, I think that was the high chair." I looked back at my mistaken suitor, who was no longer trying to warn me. Nor was he mouthing the words "You're hot." His sexy little mouth formed words closer to "You're a moron" before he sped on to a safer stretch of highway.

Mike pulled over and ascertained that we hadn't caused any traffic accidents. We said goodbye to the remaining parts of the mangled and irretrievable high chair.

"Flirting with you, my ass," Mike muttered.

"Good job tying everything down, sweetie," I replied.

* * *

CHAPTER 13

Running (Down My Leg)

When I reached the point in my life where I was hands-down positive that I would never, *ever*, for the rest of eternity, shoot-me-otherwise, be pregnant again, I decided I would run a marathon. What better way to restore some semblance of normalcy to the lunacy that had taken over my body? Running would firm, tone, and reduce. And if I have to exercise, I like running. I like that it's solitary and monotonous. Those are perks. I don't want to Zumba or Spin or punch the air in a mockery of my frailty. I don't want a cheery blonde in leg warmers clapping, screaming, and forcing Gloria Estefan on me. That's my personal version of hell.

I started with one mile, went to two, and so on. I ran a 5K and then a 10K. Eight- and ten-mile runs became events that I looked forward to. It was time on my own and the closest I could get to any form of meditation. I was excited on the morning of my first half marathon.

I parked at the finish line and boarded a bus to the start with my fellow runners. My neighbor on the bus had legs as long as I am tall.

"Are you running the marathon?" he asked.

"Half marathon," I admitted. "It's my first."

"Oh. I only run marathons," he said. I hadn't expected condescension so early in the day, before even approaching the starting line. I prefer to be demeaned in the afternoon.

The bus arrived at the park where the race would begin, and I huddled with my fellow racers for awkward and insufficient warmth. I was eager and early, as if showing up to the starting line first would make up for my later lack of speed.

The race began, and off we went. I'm slow and plodding, so a distance of 13.1 miles was sure to take in excess of two hours. After four minutes, not yet half a mile into the race, my iPod crapped, a very human failure for this tiny technological marvel. Once I accepted the fact that I would not have Eminem telling me how fucking tough I am, or the Scissor Sisters making me wish I was a young gay man in 1970s New York, I resorted to eavesdropping.

A handful of pairs ran, husband and wife duos, which you can tell because after so many years of marriage, you can't help but begin to dress alike. It happens subconsciously. One day you realize that your wardrobes are identical, save for a few variances like bras and heels. These couples had matching shirts and running hats or his-and-her sets of accessories and gear. *That's nice that they're running together*, I thought, but after listening in on the conversations of a handful of them, I noticed a common theme of the men telling the women how they should run.

"You need to slow down; you're going to wear yourself out too soon."

"You need to speed up; we're not going to make it under two hours at this pace."

I saw the women roll their eyes or pretend not to hear.

At mile three, I paused my eavesdropping because I realized I was about to pass my seatmate from the bus. He was walking, leisurely. *At mile three*. Did he take an extended break early on in order to rub his lightning speed in our faces later? He appeared in no way injured or perturbed, just a guy out for a stroll. I only run marathons, my ass.

At mile five, I began to encounter more husband and wife teams and more kvetching from the men.

"You're not drinking enough water."

"You're drinking too much water."

"Put your shoulders back."

"Lean your torso forward."

These were not running coaches or personal trainers, simply nagging husbands, the type that like to make snide and poorly disguised criticisms of their wives at dinner parties.

If I hadn't been focused so intently on the death-rattle wheeze coming from my lungs with each stride, or wondering whether the moisture running down my inner thigh was sweat or, more likely, urine, I would have bitched back at the men. *Shut the fuck up and let her run.*

I don't care how clean she demands you keep the kitchen. By telling her how she should run, the man is ultimately suggesting that he knows her body better than she does, which makes him the Adolf of all control freaks.

After recognizing with much regret that I cannot control control freaks, I turned my attention back to the matter of moisture. It seemed odd for an inordinate amount of sweat to be trickling down my inner thigh. But I certainly wasn't peeing. At least, not purposefully.

Like most mothers, I had a track record when it came to involuntary leaking. During pregnancy, it was obligatory that I peed a wee bit for every sneeze or laugh or surprise, or any kind of movement that required even a hint of strain. In full naïveté, I assumed seepage would cease when I no longer had another individual practicing their Irish step-dance on my lower hemisphere. The problem persisted after my pregnancies, especially when I sneezed. As a result, I hold sneezes in; they erupt in my head with a weird internal snort, but at least I don't wet myself.

"Doesn't that hurt?" people ask.

"Yes," I confirm. "Yes, it does."

"Why don't you just sneeze?"

"Yeah, just let it out!" they plead.

I used to say it was a lingering habit from when I was pregnant, but now I just tell them the truth.

"If I sneeze, I might pee."

That's all I need to say.

During the half marathon, there was no sneezing, nor was there an active or conscious effort of urination, but by mile eight, I was leaking fairly regularly. This had never happened during training. Much like my disappointment with other mothers for not warning me about the probe an ultrasound tech wields, I was shocked that other runners hadn't brought the possibility of this scenario to my attention. If I'm going to pee in front of hundreds of strangers who watch and clap, just as I have applauded my daughters' efforts to pee-pee in the potty, then I sure as hell want to know about it ahead of time.

I spoke to other runners after the race and learned that this was, in fact, a common occurrence for those who've given birth. After blatantly surveying their crotches, though, I can report that none of them appeared to have quite the lack of control that I did. There should be an award for that, some sort of recognition for the fact that, though I may move slower than a dying earthworm, I finish a 13.1-mile race even when I've wet my pants.

The second half marathon a month later was a much more enjoyable experience. My iPod worked, it was a women-only race, I was not overhydrated and managed to avoid urine leakage, and the finish line greeted me with champagne and chocolate. Others found this unfathomable.

"Ugh. Who would want to drink alcohol after running thirteen miles?"

The answer is simple. I would.

My love of alcohol, champagne in particular (that's a lie, I'm not really particular), trumps any minor deterrent like complete physical exhaustion and dehydration. Upon finishing the race, I immediately approached the champagne table and crouched down to get an accurate view of each plastic cup and how much liquid it contained.

The woman in charge of pouring the champagne looked alarmed and ready to administer CPR if I collapsed completely.

"I'm fine," I explained. "I'm just looking for the fullest glass."

"Oh!" She smiled, relieved. "Here, take this one." And with that, she filled a plastic cup to the rim. I don't know her name, but I love her.

After two half marathons, I determined that attempting a full marathon would result in my death. As I was not yet ready to die, I decided to keep running half marathons instead. My third and final half marathon of the summer was a bit of a letdown. It was poorly organized and required hundreds of racers to run through a narrow opening in a chain-link fence at the start, a bottleneck of rodents scurrying in mob mentality.

My knees were exceptionally crunchy the day of this race, and I ended up limping the last five miles, a pathetic shuffle that lasted long past when I should have stopped. Every now and then, a race staffer puttered by on a glorified golf cart. I assumed he was looking for bodies. By mile nine, I started fantasizing that he would motor by, calling my name.

"Amanda Turner? I'm looking for Amanda Turner?"

"I'm Amanda Turner," I'd huff.

"Ms. Turner, I'm sorry to inform you that you will absolutely not be able to finish this race, nor continue even a little bit."

"No!" I'd cry, feigning devastation.

"I'm sorry, Ms. Turner, but you must come with me immediately in my motorized vehicle."

"But . . . why?"

"I'm sorry to inform you that So-and-so has died."

So-and-so could be a close friend or relative, because in my fantasy of the moment, the death of a dear one was preferable to the prospect of actually finishing the race. As is often the case, though, my friends and family dropped the ball in their failure to drop dead. I was forced to complete the remaining four miles in a lopsided plod.

"That was a miserable, horrible, painful, and pointless experience," I told my husband. "I'm not going to try to do a full marathon, and I'm never doing that again."

"Okay," he said. "Unless they have champagne at the finish line?"

"Yes," I amended. "I might do it again if there's champagne at the finish line."

* * *

Before children and while working overseas, I had ample opportunity to try my hand at other forms of exercise, though I was never serious about getting into shape. I was still a smoker and hadn't yet developed the motivational power and disappointment of a post-pregnancy body.

In Marrakech, we lived in a hotel with both a gym and a heated pool. I figured if I had time to kill, then I might as well every once in a while move my fat butt from the indentations it had made on the couch. I'd never been much of a swimmer, but it seemed like a good time to start, especially if the pool was heated. I even bought a pair of goggles.

When I arrived, I found that the gym charged guests eight dollars for each visit. This seemed exorbitant, especially in light of the fact that after thirty minutes at a gym, I'd run screaming for the exit in search of fattening food to replenish whatever calories I might have managed to eradicate. We also were financially strapped. People incorrectly assumed that our international work was accompanied by a lavish salary, but that wasn't the case. And eight dollars was eight dollars.

No matter about the gym, I thought, *I'll stick with the pool, which is free.* As I removed the goggles from their packaging, I pictured myself merrily swimming laps every morning and afternoon, the laps that people swim in the movies. They never get completely out of breath, and they always exit the pool looking strong and refreshed and healthy. That's what I had in mind.

From the safety of our hotel room, where strangers could not point at me and laugh, I tried to put on the goggles. Thankfully, I didn't wait until I was sitting by the pool, because I found that I couldn't fit them around my head, and at one point feared that I might crush my own skull. I never thought of my head as abnormally large, but who knows? Maybe I just needed to adjust them. After verifying that these goggles were indeed meant for adults, I moved the straps out to the largest possible setting. This time I managed to fit them on my head, but they were so tight that I physically could not open my eyes, and isn't the point of goggles to allow you to open your eyes? Mike told me I simply did not adjust them properly, though I would like to note that he failed to ever show me the correct way, whatever that may be.

I abandoned the goggles and went down to the pool. There were two dozen people around the pool, but nobody actually *in* the pool. I found this quite suspect. I dipped a tentative toe. This was not a heated pool. This was a big freezing puddle that served little purpose other than an aesthetic one.

For three days, I sat by the pool, working hard on my tan and telling myself that I would go for a swim. Every now and then, one of the other guests braved the water, and they didn't scream or die or lose any appendages. On the third day, I forced myself. I went to the nearest ladder, stepped down a rung, whispered, "You're not going to die, so just fucking do it, you pussy," and jumped. Yes, it was cold, but as I had speculated, I did not die.

I have never been a strong swimmer. My swimming ability is most comparable to the grace I display when riding a bike. I cannot ride a bike. My first memories of swimming are with my sister. She would calmly support me and instruct me how to float on my back, but I would inevitably panic and climb up her in an attempt to perch myself on the top of her head.

Until I experienced laser eye surgery a few years ago, I was never comfortable in the water. My vision was extremely poor, and taking off my glasses required heavy dependence on other senses and people. There have been those who have implied that this is a lame excuse for not enjoying the water, but seriously, lack of vision while frolicking in a pool or the ocean is not fun and even a little scary. That's why everyone cheats at Marco Polo.

As I pondered the temperature, I realized that I must have entered the pool at its deepest point. While treading water, I recalled a particular day at swimming lessons when I was a child. I remembered doggy paddling about and mistakenly ending up in the deep end (probably because I couldn't see where I was going). As I struggled to stay afloat and swallowed gallons of pool water, in which my classmates had undoubtedly peed, one of the older girls swam over to me. Her name was something stupid like Topsy, and as she smoothly glided in my direction with perfected strokes, I felt relief. I thought she was there to help me over to the edge. But instead, she paused, expertly treading water just out of my grasp.

"Miss Lisa says you shouldn't be in the deep area, and she wants you to go back to the other side of the pool." As soon as she delivered her message, she turned and swam away.

"No shit, you condescending bitch. Help me!" But no, I didn't really say that. I actually gasped and spluttered something more along the lines of "Okay, Topsy, thanks. Yeah, that's cool." My struggle to the side of the pool felt like an undertaking in which I might die, and I pictured Miss Lisa and Topsy giggling together at my plight, off-handedly wondering whether or not I'd make it.

The only other swimming memory I have is when my grandparents took my mother and me to spend an afternoon at a German club of which they were members. I'd found some other girls my age, and we were jumping off the edge of the pool, spinning in the air before we hit the water. This was great fun and the type of activity children begin and are then compelled to continue until physical exhaustion sets in or, of course, until someone spins around in midair without having jumped far enough, thereby splitting their chin open on the way down on the edge of the pool. I was the child who managed to do this.

I dragged myself from the pool, sobbing and scared by the blood on my hands. A grandfather of one of the other children was nearby. For a second, I thought he would comfort me, bleeding and distraught as I was, and maybe help me make my way back to my family. Instead, he pointed at me and spoke to his own granddaughter.

"You see," he scolded her. "*That's* how you could get hurt, and *that's* why I didn't want you jumping off the edge of the pool." With that, he grabbed the little girl by the arm and dragged her away.

As I treaded water in Marrakech, I forced Miss Lisa and Topsy and uncaring old men from my mind. I wasn't just a few feet from touching the bottom; it seemed *miles* away. I decided to make my way to a more shallow area. I swam underwater for a bit, then above, then on my back. Figuring I'd covered some distance, I resumed treading water to gain my bearings. I had traveled approximately five feet from where I'd entered the pool. Not only had I not made it very far, but I was still many feet away from being able to touch the bottom. *I'm not tired*, I told myself. *Look cool; look casual.*

At that point, I could have swum to the closest wall and had a little rest, but I was determined to look like I was enjoying myself and make it back to where I'd entered. Nothing screams Confident, Competent Woman-in-Water like the doggy paddle, so I tried that again. It was far more exhausting than Labradors make it appear, that's for damn sure. When I was near exhaustion, I switched to long, smooth strokes above the water, which I'm sure has a technical name, but I just think of as How Normal People Swim. This, too, proved difficult. I turned to my back and considered drowning myself just to be done with the whole mess. Instead, I went back to brief intervals of doggy paddle and How Normal People Swim. Eventually, and with the knowledge and acceptance of this failed experience, I made it back to the ladder. I tried to stifle the sound of my breathing, which included huge, panicked gasps for air and drew looks from the poolside guests. My total time in the water could not have been more than three minutes. I was exhausted. These were not the leisurely laps I'd pictured. I did not go back in the pool.

My abilities did not improve over time, and it was clear when I became a parent that I'd be useless when it came time to teach our girls to swim, or even enjoy the water with them. This was problematic because Idaho summers necessitate pools to keep children from shriveling up into sweat-soaked, red-faced demons.

"Mama, are we going swimming today?" Emilia asked.

"I don't know; you have to ask your father."

"Why?"

"Because Mommy doesn't swim."

"But I thought you love me," she said, seconds from tears.

"I'm sorry, honey. Mommy's a cat in water."

"You're a cat?" And with that, I successfully distracted her enough until Daddy could address the swimming issue.

I'm as good at biking as I am at swimming. The last time I rode a bike was in Mexico. Friends were planning to hike up an arroyo and wanted to know if I would like to join them. *Great*, I thought, *I love a good hike.* Then someone casually mentioned that they were going to take their bikes to ride the first part of the hike, and they had one that I could borrow. *Fine*, I thought, *I can do this.* After all, I was by far the youngest of the six-person group; in some cases, decades younger. Surely I could keep up.

We drove roughly an hour to get to the starting point of our bike/hike, so there was no possibility of saying, "You know what, I really need to get some laundry done, so I'm going to head back." The first part of the biking was, to me, the equivalent of jumping off a cliff. *Why not just hurl my body over the edge?* I wondered. The bike was merely an extra item to land on top of my crumpled form in case I wasn't injured enough by the time I reached the bottom. I watched the others go and figured I had no other option. I crashed twice, but I didn't die or break anything. One of my companions confided in me that we had just done the most treacherous part. *Good*, I thought, *because if it gets any worse than that, I might as well start smashing my head in with a rock right now.*

The rest of the journey by bike was not as dangerous but certainly demanding. In some areas, the dirt gave way to sand. Actually, I liked the sand, because it provided the least painful and embarrassing way to stop. My usual means of stopping involved searching for something to crash into. At various legs of the trip, my companions would try to ride through the sand, but the only person who has mastered this is my father-in-law. He is a compact man who grows devilishly excited when any sort of challenge is presented to him. He rides along and bellows out a maniacal battle cry as he approaches the sand, at which point he begins pedaling as fast as his legs allow. This technique results in very slow movement, but as others give up or fall to the side, he perseveres until he crosses the length of sand. At the other side, he cries out "AHA!" in triumph. And he proudly recounts the story for days to come.

Periodically throughout the rest of the biking, my companions would ride next to me, giving me the opportunity to ask questions like, "How do you shift?" and "Which brake should I use again?" and "What gear would you say a person should be in about now?" Eventually they set my gears to a certain level and told me not to touch them. When the biking portion was finished, we began the hike, during which I secretly hoped a rattlesnake would bite me, because surely that would get me out of having to get back on the bike for the return trek. Sadly, I did not encounter a rattlesnake.

Biking was yet another activity that fell squarely on Mike's shoulders when we became parents, and I informed him of this in no uncertain terms.

"You don't think it's important for our children to know how to swim and ride a bike?" Mike asked.

"That's not what I said. I said it's up to *you* to teach them those things. I'll handle what I'm good at, and you handle what you're good at."

"So you're going to teach them . . . ?" he baited.

"Well, apparently I'm going to teach them how not to be an asshole, because you just lost rights to that one."

"I was just kidding," he amended. "I know you're good at lots of things."

"Start naming them," I demanded.

"Reading? Cleaning?"

"Good, but give me one more."

He thought for a moment, and I could tell "drinking" was on the tip of his tongue.

"You make a killer bloody Mary?"

Saved.

"Okay," I relented, "you're off the hook."

"So, I have to teach the girls how to swim and ride a bike, and you're going to teach them how to read, clean, and make a bloody?"

"Yes," I agreed. "The parental bases are officially covered."

* * *

CHAPTER 14

And You Smell Like One, Too

Once you reach parenthood, you automatically become a participant in a new sport, whether you are willing or not, called The Birthday Party. No matter how much you train for The Birthday Party, you will lose.

Where you hold The Birthday Party, how much you spend, and who you invite all contribute to how much of a failure you will be as a parent and how much you will disappoint your child. If your children later do heroin, it is because you fucked up The Birthday Party. And whether or not the children have fun is not as important as whether or not you rented a bouncy house and if you made your cake from scratch.

When it comes to birthday parties, I proudly confess that I have made nearly every mistake one can make. I've failed to invite close friends, scheduled a beach party when it was too cold, and I usually serve beer. It's not as if I *only* serve beer. It's not as if I present a toddler with their first lager. I have juice boxes on hand as well, but I see no reason to deprive the adults of a nice amber or Hefeweizen. In fact, if there is ever a time when a parent is in need of alcoholic assistance, it's at an infant or toddler's birthday party. I wasn't slinging manhattans or mudslides, so I don't see what the big deal is.

Because Emilia was born on Memorial Day and her birthday always falls in close proximity to the holiday weekend, she is often disappointed by the friends who are out of town on family vacations and can't make it to her party. We still managed to throw a good-sized bash on her first birthday, complete with presents, balloons, streamers, kiddie pools, and a bubble machine. This is when parents go all out, on the birthday that the child will not remember or ever give a damn about. But the parents know that a celebration is warranted, an acknowledgment of surviving that first treacherous year with a first child.

Ivy suffered from second-child syndrome. Her first birthday party was not actually a party. This wasn't pure laziness, only partial laziness, coupled with the fact that I was counting on her not remembering or ever giving a damn about it.

She was teething and miserable at the time, and money was tight. Instead of a party, I bought a five-dollar pizza and some secondhand toys. We went to the park, no guests invited. She couldn't eat the pizza because of her swollen gums, and she hated the toys I bought, no doubt smelling the secondhand store stench clinging to them. By the time she's old enough to read this, I will have made it up to her.

Boise is a city filled with wonderful parks and picnic areas. If the weather is decent, there is no reason to spend five hundred dollars renting a big obnoxious facility with an indoor playground. There are plenty of big obnoxious outdoor playgrounds that are free, though dueling birthday parties can cause a fair amount of preschooler conflict.

I took my girls to the third birthday party of one of their friends at one such playground. All of the kids had a wonderful time falling off of the jungle gyms, getting sunburned, and making themselves ill by consuming mass quantities of frosting. The excitement reached a high when a party rental company showed up and began setting up a large bouncy house. It was the deluxe model, a twenty-foot Batman bouncy house with basketball add-on, interior obstacle course, and a slide that shoots lasers at you on the way down.

"Yay! Bouncy house! Bouncy house!" The children ran toward it, screaming and joyful, only to have their hopes and dreams crushed. A woman stood in front of the growing inflatable, trying to block it with outstretched arms.

"I'm sorry," she said to the kids, "but this isn't for your party."

The three-year-olds, including the birthday girl, looked back at the birthday girl's mom as if she'd just kicked a puppy.

"Who wants more cake?" she asked. "Did everyone get their party favors?"

The other problem with public parks is the party crasher, the kid who's a little older and rougher, with parents nowhere to be found. The party crasher is usually male, though not always, and he helps himself to food and toys and gives out the occasional beating. You want to grab him by the scruff of the neck and drag him off to juvie, but you're a teensy bit afraid of him yourself, as you see definite potential for a future serial killer.

The problem *girls* take a much more passive-aggressive approach. They poke and prod at their prey over the course of an hour. When the other child finally reacts, they set their lower lip to a quiver and with tearful, wide eyes, claim, "Mommy, that mean boy hit me." These same girls are likely to introduce themselves as princesses, as in, "My name is Princess Penelope." They are adept at ruining social functions, and everyone present can see that the princess is a little asshole, with the exception of the little asshole's parents, because they are assholes themselves.

* * *

My niece attended a birthday party at an upscale, downtown hair salon. Not an upscale salon for children, but the type of salon where you spend a few hundred dollars per appointment and the walls are decorated with blown-up photographs of emaciated supermodels with smears of heavy makeup and ironically scraggly hair. Am I the only one who's noticed this? That hair salons display pictures of supermodels with really atrocious hair? Maybe that's how they get us to think they've done such a good job. When we see our new hairstyle in the mirror, we see it against the backdrop of photographs depicting frizzy and shellacked maelstroms of stylists gone bad. And is an environment of scissors, straight razors, curling irons, and chemicals really the best choice for a child's birthday party? More importantly, will they serve wine for the parents?

That same niece, who was a social butterfly at the age of six and attended a ridiculous number of upscale birthday parties, also attended a Princess Ballerina Birthday Party. Her father, unshaven and clad in sweats, delivered her to the party to find that it took place at a dance studio downtown. Professional ballerinas greeted them as they entered a great hall where fifteen tables, each seating eight, were set with fine china. Flocks of little girls flitted about in full Texas-beauty-pageant getup.

"Maybe we should have combed your hair," said the dad. He smiled self-consciously at the other more manicured parents.

"Look, Dad, there's a barre!" screamed his daughter. She ran to the ballet barre, across the length of the room. "You always complain that these birthday parties don't have a bar, but this one does!"

The moment could only have been perfected further if a plastic flask had fallen from the waistband of his sweatpants.

* * *

Birthdays become more complicated as time goes on. One year, Emilia wanted a new puzzle for her birthday. Done! The next year she was a little more demanding.

"Mama, I'm gonna be four! I'm so excited!"

"Me, too!" I said.

"Mama, I want a birthday cake," she informed me.

"Of course we'll have a birthday cake," I assured her.

"Not cupcakes," she said.

"Oh." I realized she had me figured out. I liked cupcakes; they were one size fits all, easy to buy, and required no cutting.

"No cupcakes," she repeated. "I want a birthday cake."

"Okay," I agreed.

"And I want a lion cake."

"What?"

"And not a mean lion and not a scary lion. I want a happy lion cake."

"A happy lion cake?"

"Okay, Mama? No cupcakes!"

"Okay, okay, no cupcakes."

I contemplated buying a lion figurine and plopping it onto the frosting of a store-bought cake.

"And you *make* the lion, Mama. You don't put the lion on the cake, you *make* the lion. Okay, Mama?"

I almost gave her a time-out for reading my mind.

For my daughters, time is marked not by seasons, but by birthdays and holidays. These are the epic events that promise various forms of sugar and a senseless amount of money spent on plastic crap. One Christmas, in an attempt to have more of a family experience and less plastic, we decided to take them on a train to the North Pole (otherwise known as Banks, Idaho). My daughters were enamored with trains. They didn't like dolls or stuffed animals or pretty dresses, but they loved trains. It was an hour-long drive to the train station, where we boarded a passenger car, cramming in behind tiny tables of chipped linoleum and stains from the seventies. It was freezing and cramped, and Ivy screamed every time she caught a glimpse of one of the elves. But let's be honest, elves are creepy.

"I don't mean to be the pessimist," I said to Mike, realizing that this family experience was a terrible idea, "but how the hell are we going to survive a three-hour ride on this thing? I didn't even bring a flask."

"I'm going on a recon mission," Mike said.

Mike always thinks that he can find a better spot. I never believe him, and he is always right. He abandoned me with our squirming offspring, and I was dismayed to realize that I'd gone through all of our emergency treats and the train was not yet moving.

Ivy kept dropping her pacifier and then demanding its return with a fury we'd come to know well. I'd been a mom long enough to have given up on trying to cleanse it. She'd be chewing on the carpet before the trip was over, in any case.

Mike returned to the train car, my knight in shining fleece, and said, "Follow me and look natural."

We herded our way through the throngs and three other train cars before entering the second to last one. Not only was it warmer, but also less crowded. My heart skipped a beat as I looked to the end of the car where a woman staffed a bar, lacing coffee drinks with copious amounts of booze. I gazed at Mike and whispered, "My hero."

Once the train was moving, the kids were happy. Once we had our drinks, we were happy. Mr. and Mrs. Claus came through, as did carolers with surprising talent. I don't know why, but I'd expected them to suck.

We reached the North Pole, where we disembarked and were first in line for Santa. Emilia sat on his lap and told him that she wanted a big red flashlight. Ivy sat on his lap, punched him in the groin, and tried to rip his face off.

* * *

At Easter, we developed the ingenious plan of faking a knock at the door and opening it to find the children's Easter baskets.

"Oh, look! The Easter bunny brought baskets for Emilia and Ivy!" Mike and I chimed as we opened the door. Instead of viewing the baskets with joy, they trampled them and attempted to charge into the street to get a look at the departing Easter bunny.

"Easter bunny!" Emilia called, looking up and down the street.

"Bunny!" Ivy demanded.

"I think the Easter bunny is gone," I said.

"But look at the Easter baskets he left for you," Mike added. The children ignored us.

"You're implying the Easter bunny is male," I whispered to Mike.

"Oh, please," he said. "The Easter bunny is definitely a boy bunny."

"What makes you sure?" I challenged.

"Hello? Peter Rabbit? Everyone knows the Easter bunny is a boy."

"Wait," I said. "Peter Rabbit is the Easter bunny? I'm not sure if I knew that."

"What rock did you grow up under?" he asked.

Before I could make the Beatrix Potter case, we turned our attention back to the children. Throughout this conversation, Emilia cupped her hands around her mouth and repeatedly called, "Easter bunny? Come back!"

"Bunny! Back!" Ivy commanded.

"Girls, come look at the baskets," I pleaded.

"Yeah, the Easter bunny had to go," Mike said.

"No," Emilia said. "We just need to find him."

"Bunny?" Ivy uttered a final plea.

We now refer to Easter as The Sunday of Endless Tears.

When my children did see the Easter bunny, which I arranged in recompense for The Sunday of Endless Tears, they screamed and cried and ran in fear. The only positive thing about Easter, in their estimation, was the abundance of "baby eggs," also known as jelly beans. This makes sense, it being such a biologically confused holiday of rabbits and eggs.

Holidays that were primarily for adults lost all meaning

and significance for us. Most New Year's Eves find us in bed by 9:30. (We'd go to bed earlier, but we have to wait for the kids to fall asleep.) St. Patrick's Day is nothing more than a time when I hide my family indoors in fear of drunk drivers. At best, I'll have a Guinness while doing the dishes.

The romance of Valentine's Day is a long-lost memory, replaced now with either guilt over the fact that I forgot to forge Valentines from my toddlers to their classmates, who can't read them anyway, or spent furiously attempting to create said Valentines in the hopes of avoiding Bad Parent status.

Why should Valentine's Day be celebrated in schools and day cares anyway? Isn't it about getting liquored up and mushy at overpriced dinners? Isn't it a time to indulge in champagne and chocolate truffles? Shouldn't the focus be on guaranteeing that overwrought couples get laid on this one night of the year?

The Fourth of July is shitty for everyone, because mixing fireworks in with the general population is stupid. One need only read the headlines on the fifth of July to verify this. Inevitably, there are a handful of deaths from people who thought it wise to place fireworks on their heads or see how many fireworks they could light at the same time in their driveway. It's an evening of intense anxiety for dogs and veterans. Emilia gets burned by sparklers from packages touting their safety for kids, and Ivy spends hours with her hands clamped over her ears. Instead of calling it the Fourth of July, how about The Day for Drunk Boys to Play with Things Loud and Dangerous?

October brings the dependable disappointment of Halloween, spent hiding in a darkened home from rude teenagers who think that trick-or-treating past the age of thirteen is acceptable. The day after Halloween is even worse, with the carnage of murdered pumpkins littering the streets for all to see. Explaining the violence of victimized jack-o'-lanterns to a three-year-old is something I'd never anticipated. That said, I'm a big fan of costumes. As babies, I'd dress the girls as cows and lobsters, in adorable one-pieces that they'd wear with looks of confusion, wondering why Mommy couldn't stop laughing at them. As they got older, I'd let them have input as to what they wanted to be on Halloween. Without fail, I'd get excited about making epic costumes for them. This involved me spending a small fortune at a craft store, then realizing over the following week that I have no talent when it comes to sewing, design, or construction. In a pinch, though, I can hold a costume together if I have four hundred safety pins handy.

Thanksgiving has easily become my favorite holiday. We have family time, good food and wine, and we forgo the pressure of wondering for whom we forgot to buy a gift or mail a card. There are no mythical figures or creatures to frighten the children, and it does not require middle-of-the-night staging, tacky decorations, or waking at the butt crack of dawn.

It's a time to reflect and focus on what is really important. Namely, the meal. To me, Thanksgiving is one gigantic, all-day dinner party. It's about turkey and stuffing, gravy and mashed potatoes, and heated pumpkin pie. It's a time to enjoy bloody Marys and mimosas in the morning, a few midday beers, wine in the evening, and martinis and coffee cocktails at night. The kids build forts in the living room, and the adults play cards into the wee hours.

Most of all, Thanksgiving is about being thankful and mildly drunk at the same time.

Mike demonstrated this beautifully one year at a family

Thanksgiving at the home of relatives in Walla Walla. I'd been changing diapers in another room and preparing the kids for bed. When I returned to the dining room, I found that Mike had gone beyond "mildly" drunk. He held the other adults hostage in conversation at the dinner table.

"Here she is," he slurred as I entered the room. "You all just don't understand how awesome she is. My wife is so awesome. Seriously, I want everyone here to tell her how fucking awesome she is." I was touched by both his enthusiasm and eloquence. These family moments are what Thanksgiving is all about.

* * *

CHAPTER 15

I'll Be with You in Just a Miggot

I've always thought it important to record as much of what my children say as possible. From the time they learn to talk, kids use their words to embarrass and entertain us, and I couldn't make this stuff up.

Emilia and I sat together in our driveway, alternately drawing with sidewalk chalk and reading books about adventurous animals. Sometimes my children tell me stories, which is always a treat. Every story begins with "One day" and ends with "The end." What takes place in the middle may or may not be coherent.

"Mama," Emilia said, "the weather is so happy!"

"Yes," I agreed, "the weather *is* happy."

It was the first good weather we'd had for some time, so people were out walking dogs, riding bikes, and chatting with neighbors. A woman walked alone up the street. I couldn't tell her age from where I sat, other than to say she was somewhere between twenty and sixty, and this I gained from her posture and presence alone. She wore a long, plain skirt and a wide-brimmed, woven hat. From our driveway, and at the top of her three-year-old lungs, Emilia shouted, "Mama, look at the grandmother!"

I reached for the nearest Sandra Boynton book, pretending I somehow hadn't heard the statement my daughter had just bellowed an inch from my ear.

"*One hippo all alone, calls two hippos on the phone,*" I read, keeping my eyes on the page. "Emilia," I whispered, "read the book with me." I continued in a louder voice: "*Three hippos at the door, bring along another four.*"

Disappointed with my lack of response, Emilia addressed the woman directly.

"Hey!" she yelled. "You a grandmother!"

"*All the hippos go BERSERK!*" I continued reading. Barring any severe hearing impairment, I'm sure the woman heard. I don't know whether or not she was offended, as I was too chicken to look up. Instead, I waded through the Boynton library, reading about partying hippos, hippos who love their belly buttons, and personal penguins, waiting for the woman to be out of sight so that we could steal away inside.

* * *

When I have no makeup and bedhead and haven't yet brushed my teeth, Emilia would say, with genuine sincerity and immeasurable enthusiasm, "Mama, you look beautiful!"

When my toes, which are naturally as hairy as a hobbit's, have no polish, sizable calluses, and bits of lint embedded under the nails, she'd say, "Mama! I love your toes!"

While Emilia doled out the compliments left and right, Ivy was very focused on giving people things. If you set down a beverage, for instance, Ivy would immediately pick it up and give it back to you, which often resulted in an unplanned laundry night.

"Mama, that's your milk?" Emilia asked, as Ivy ran as fast as her dimpled legs allowed, trying to get to my wineglass so that she could "give it to me" before I moved it out of reach.

"Yep, that's Mommy's," I said, reaching the wine before Ivy did, but still managing to slosh most of it on myself and the couch.

"You know what to say, Mama?" Emilia asked.

"What's that, Emilia?" as I fumbled with a pack of baby wipes, which make excellent cleaning agents but aren't very absorbent when it comes to red wine.

"There's no use to cry on the milk spill," she asserted.

* * *

My daughters are often far too outgoing, saying hello not only to strangers and animals, but also to headless mannequins we pass in the mall. Everything is exciting and merits a "Whoa!" As we drive through town, they'll point out the window and scream, "Whoa! A bird!" as if they've just sighted Dora the Explorer, live and in the flesh.

Most of their utterances are organic, like when Emilia would reach her arms as high as she could, and say, "Mama, I can't reach the sky. It's too tall." Others are my doing. I taught both my children that a cat says "meow," a cow says "moo," and a giraffe says "I'm tall."

The first time Emilia threw up, she was baffled, not knowing what had happened to her body or how to describe it.

"Mama," she said, "I coughed, and I spilled my cough." The second time, she told me that she had "a really big sneeze!"

She went through a phase of being very curious about apples, and by "apples" she meant "nipples." I tried to communicate to her that it is not appropriate to tell someone you are going to tickle their nipples or their apples, but she didn't believe me.

When it comes to language, it's hard to break a habit that a child is convinced is correct. I know this firsthand, as I insisted for years that my teddy bear, who came with the name Pot Belly Bear, was Hot Belly Bear. Hot Belly simply made more sense; I'd never heard the term Pot Belly. Whenever anyone tried to tell me that his name was really Pot Belly Bear, I assumed they were trying to trick me, and what kind of a moron did they think I was?

Emilia at a similar age decided that her favorite treat was chocolate hooding. She had no trouble forming a "p" sound yet insisted that chocolate "hooding" was the best thing since television.

When we'd ask her to do something and she wasn't ready, she'd tell us to "Wait just a miggot."

"Emilia, can you say 'minute'?"

"Miggot."

"Minute?"

"Miggot."

We'd volley this back and forth a few miggots and I'd resign myself to it, silently placing the blame squarely with my husband's side of the family.

"Good job," I'd say.

Then she'd run off in search of her sister, screaming in sing-song threat, "Ivy, here I come! I'm gonna tickle your apples!"

They enjoy musical instruments but for the longest time didn't grasp the concept of the *instruments* making the music. Instead, they'd hold whistles an inch away from their mouths and sing an extended note.

"Ooooohh."

"Girls, watch," I instructed. "Put the whistle in your mouth and blow into it. Watch Mommy."

"No, Mama," Emilia corrected me. "You don't do it right. We learned it at school. We know how to do it." As if they'd rehearsed it a million times, they held their whistles up to their faces, but not touching their lips, and sang in unison a high-pitched "Ooooohh."

By "school," Emilia meant day care, and I wondered if not actually touching their mouths to a whistle was taught to curb the sharing of germs. Day care also included karate lessons, which I was most excited about because I wanted to see how adorable my kids would look in tiny white gis.

After Emilia participated in a few karate lessons, we asked her for a demonstration.

"Emilia," Mike asked, "what did you learn in karate today?"

We both braced ourselves, expecting a good swift kick to the shins or a fist in the gut. Instead, she snapped into perfect posture and barked, "Yes, sir!"

"Holy shit." I looked at Mike.

"That's money well spent, right there," he said.

As time went on, we asked for a more physical demonstration, and all she showed us was a "round kick," which was a flailing leg that took her off balance and ended with her falling down.

"Good job!" we cheered.

Another month passed, and we again asked what she learned in karate.

"Mama"—she looked me dead in the eye—"I have knowledge in my head, strength in my body, and honor in my heart."

"Holy shit is right," Mike muttered.

I left work on occasion to sneak into day care and spy on the karate class without being seen. It was a mix of serious technique and pure silliness. With an extended leg, the kids chanted, "Hey, bad guys, smell my feet!" Money well spent.

* * *

In the mornings, it is painfully obvious which child takes after which parent. While Mike and Ivy rise at five in the morning, Emilia and I would sleep until ten if permitted. In terms of temperament, though, Ivy takes after me, and Emilia takes after Mike. This means that when Ivy wakes at dawn, because she is an early riser like her father, she also wakes up grumpy, with a lack of morning cheer. It would be useless for me to deny where that comes from.

Emilia, on the other hand, has her father's disposition. On occasion, I'll go into her room to wake her, at which point she goes from a dead sleep to sitting bolt upright and proclaims, "Mama! I'm so happy!"

Other early morning announcements include, "Nana and Grammy are coming to play with me!" Both Nana and Grammy live approximately three thousand miles away, in different directions, so I later call both my mother and my mother-in-law and tell them what Emilia has said in the hopes of guiling them into a visit, during which we will fully exploit their babysitting capabilities.

My mother (Grammy), my mother-in-law (Nana), and I all miraculously enjoy one another's company. We fully admit that alcohol is the binding agent in our relationships. Both Grammy and Nana stayed with the girls while Mike and I took a delayed tenth wedding anniversary vacation to Ireland, by way of Amsterdam. It was delayed because, at the time of our tenth wedding anniversary, I was about to give birth to Ivy. After having been through two successful pregnancies, I can assert that a vacation while pregnant fucking sucks. So, we took our big vacation on our *eleventh* wedding anniversary when the girls were three and one, so that I might fully indulge without guilt. When I can't fully indulge, I'm a bitch. When I can only indulge with guilt, I'm a bitch. Really, my indulgence is for the good of the community.

Grammy and Nana showed up a few days before our departure to learn the routines of day care, nap time, mealtime, bedtime, and bath time. Within twenty-four hours of their arrival, Mike and I were compiling lists of rules for them to follow in the interests of our children's safety. They were as follows:

1. Do not bathe the children when you are drunk. Wait until after the children have gone to sleep to get drunk. If you are drunk before the children go to sleep, SKIP THE BATH!

2. You must keep the baby gate closed at all times. If you do not close the gate, Ivy will plummet, and if she survives, she'll likely suffer permanent physical damage. Not only will we, your children, never forgive you, but we

will also require you to aid in her care for the rest of all of our natural lives.

3. Do not feed the children and then sit out on the deck with a cocktail. You must be in the room while the children are eating. You must be conscious, attentive, and ready to administer CPR and/or the Heimlich if needed. Do not give the children jalapeños, Tabasco, or Sriracha. Do not give the children knives. You are the adults, and you must cut their food for them.

4. We have left you with a sheet of phone numbers for neighbors, day care, and the pediatrician. The most important number is 9-1-1. If you have a problem, dial 9-1-1. Do not email us to let us know that someone has a fever of 107 degrees. Call 9-1-1.

5. We love you and we are so grateful for this opportunity and we have all the confidence of the world in you. Relax, have fun, and we'll bring back souvenirs.

Any fears I harbored regarding Emilia and Ivy's safety were, of course, tempered by the fact that I could think of no two people on the planet whom I'd rather have care for our children in our absence. Nana and Grammy kept the girls both alive and happy, no small feat considering that Mike and I often content ourselves with just the former.

The experience made me grateful I was no longer the bitch I had been in my late teens. I used to think that family was something to be tolerated, not enjoyed. The bitch that I am in my thirties is far more caring.

* * *

CHAPTER 16

The Night Fury

During The Night Fury years, the difficulty of getting up in the middle of the night varied depending on my level of sobriety and how deeply I was sleeping when woken. If I was sleeping deeply *and* threw back a few drinks before bed, I was likely to wake with confusion. The knowledge that I had to function as a parent lurked somewhere within the fog of my head.

On a typical Night Fury night, I made my way out of my bedroom and into the hall, where I tripped over the fucking push-me-popper. This is one of those obnoxious toys that's been around since the dawn of plastic and makes a ridiculous amount of noise, and yet I was still compelled to purchase one for my children.

The classic version of a push-me-popper is a long, plastic blue handle from which a child navigates a clear plastic dome on red wheels. The dome is filled with multicolored balls that bounce around with an ungodly racket as the child rolls it along the floor.

I am convinced that the push-me-popper and select other toys are alive and move around of their own accord when we're not looking, just like Buzz and Woody. The push-me-popper, in particular, lurked in the shadows on nights when I'd paid a few visits to the liquor cabinet, and then it inched its way into the center of the hallway, hoping to take me down in the middle of the night. I'd thought about throwing it away, but I grew up with movies like *Child's Play* and know what demon toys are capable of, so I choose instead to live in fear.

I survived the push-me-popper and opened the door to Ivy's room, only to realize that Ivy *had* been sleeping soundly. Emilia was the one in distress, though by then, with all the commotion, they were both crying.

"Mike," I called across the hall, in the loudest whisper possible, as if there was anyone left in danger of waking, "this is going to require a Two Parent Response."

"Coming," he mumbled.

I proceeded to Ivy and lifted her out of her crib. She was irate and pooping. I had to turn on the overhead light; it would be a long time before getting her back to sleep.

On his way to comfort Emilia, Mike navigated around the push-me-popper only to step on a McDonald's Happy Meal toy. This left him bleeding with a plastic unicorn protruding grotesquely from his foot. He tried not to curse and was finally bedside, there to comfort Emilia, when he looked down and realized that he was stark naked, which was a problem, as she was three and very curious about "parts." He swiped her blanket to cover his privates, which caused her greater distress, and fled to find me in Ivy's room.

"I'll do the diaper," he said. "Will you go take care of Emilia?"

"Of course," I agreed. This meant that I would likely get back to bed long before he would.

As we switched places, he plucked the plastic unicorn from his foot. I didn't comment but silently noted that this confirmed my theory of demon toys that come alive.

I left Mike to change Ivy's diaper, which was no easy task. She was determined to launch herself off of the changing table.

"Are you okay, sweetie?" I asked Emilia. She'd mostly calmed herself down by that point, tired of waiting for parental comfort.

"I closed my eyes and saw the sea monster and the house is blowing away and the big bad wolf," she explained.

"It's okay, it was just a dream," I said.

"I *know*, Mama." She sounded exasperated. "I'm going to sleep now, so you just go you (sic) back to bed," she ordered.

I followed directions and wondered how on earth anyone ever survives with more than two children. Lying in bed, I heard the creak of the floor in Ivy's room; it was the sound of Mike rocking from foot to foot, trying to get her back down. There was a little bit of guilt as I snuggled in, but not enough to get me back out of bed. It sounded like he was on the right track, anyway.

It was one-thirty in the morning. We would likely each be up at least one more time, taking a turn with Ivy. Before I drifted off, determined to take advantage of each minute allowed to me, I contemplated the phrase, "Sleeping like a baby." Whatever moron came up with that phrase never had to contend with a Night Fury.

* * *

When Emilia was born, I thought I understood sleep deprivation. We were tired, but at nine months she began sleeping through the night, often for twelve-hour stretches. By the age of three, she was consistently announcing her bedtime.

We'd have family movie night and she would get up off of the couch, walk to the television, turn it off in the middle of the movie, and then announce to the room, "I'm tired, and I need to go to bed." She would then march down the hall while I put down my wineglass and chased after her, mumbling, "Don't you want me to tuck you in?" Usually the answer was yes, but every now and then she'd say, "No, Mama, I don't need you to tuck me in, you just go you (sic) away." I believe she inherited my sentimentality.

Most nights Emilia would go to sleep, and we wouldn't hear from her until the next morning, but occasionally we'd get a little resistance in the form of "needs." There are the classics: "I need a drink of water" and "I need you to tuck me in again." If she'd exhausted these and still resisted sleep, her creativity kicked in.

"Mama?"

"Yes, Emilia." I opened her door. "What is it?"

"I need you to clean the sand out of my belly button."

Another night, ten minutes after being tucked in, she sounded a bit more frantic. "Mama! Mama!"

"What's wrong?" I rushed to her bedside.

"I need you to tickle my armpit." With that, she hiked up her shirt and presented me with her armpit.

When Ivy came along, we believed that, like her sister, she would begin sleeping through the night around nine months. *Certainly* by a year. Emilia was a false-advertising baby.

For the first three years of her life, when Ivy woke in the wee hours, it was not with fear or sadness or the need for emotional comfort. It was with pure fury. I believe that if she'd had a fully formed vocabulary, she would have said, "I hate you, and you're ruining my life" as she clawed at our faces in an attempt to draw blood. It was one thing to deal with The Night Fury when sleep deprived, but an entirely different matter when sleep deprived and hovering between still drunk and hung over.

Mike and I went beyond our usual maintenance drinking one night after the girls were in bed. Ivy had miraculously been downgraded from The Night Fury to mere Fusspot after sleeping through the night for two nights in a row. We made the classic mistake of believing we'd entered a new phase. We stayed up too late, drinking and talking and pretending we were out on a date, free of our parental responsibilities. We finally went to bed just after midnight with the leaden body stupor that accompanies overconsumption. Midnight seems pathetically early to most people, but that's what parenthood does, it makes you pathetic. Twenty minutes later, The Night Fury returned to us in full and dreaded force. Mike and I elbowed each other for a few minutes before both getting up.

Other parents suggested that she just needed to "cry it out." I'm familiar with this tactic and used it on both of my children, but Ivy's resolve was unparalleled. She simply out-willed us. Whereas Emilia would give up after ten minutes and drift off, Ivy would last for hours. She would not tire and go to sleep. Instead, her fury built, and if we tried to wait her out, we'd simply have a more irate infant to deal with than if we'd just gotten up with her initially.

The only remedy for The Night Fury was to hold her tight

against your chest and vigorously speed walk, adding a significant bounce to each step, in circles around our kitchen and living room. I began doing this while Mike slathered some Orajel on her gums as I quickly walked by. He held the ibuprofen at the ready in case it, too, was needed. We'd used more Orajel and ibuprofen on our child than could possibly have been necessary. I know this is wrong and makes me both a bad person and parent, but when you're desperate, you'll try whatever you can. I hadn't yet tried handing her a shot of whiskey, but I was close.

After about eight laps around the kitchen, she stopped screaming but stared at me intently, daring me to slow or stop, assuring me that, if I did so, The Fury would return in full force. The problem with continuing was my increasing nausea. Running in circles is a surefire way to get queasy, but the point of actual sickness comes twice as fast when intoxicated.

"Mike, I need you to take over," I said on a pass through the kitchen.

"Okay," he said, and I handed The Night Fury off to him on the next go-around. While Mike didn't have any nausea to contend with, his ability to speed walk/bounce without colliding into walls and furniture was severely compromised. Luckily, these collisions appeased The Night Fury; she seemed to enjoy them, and after a mere forty-five minutes of relay speed walking, we were able to put her back to bed and go back to sleep ourselves. I'm convinced that Ivy knew of our impaired state. Or perhaps she found the staggered speed walking so enjoyable that she wanted to repeat the experience, over and over again. She slept in twenty-minute increments that night, waking us a dozen times with a familiar howl, until 4:30 a.m., when we gave up and put on a movie.

When I'd tell stories of The Night Fury to other parents, they were always quick to identify a solution, one that they presumed us too stupid to think of.

"Did you check her diaper?"

"Was she too hot? Was she too cold?"

"Was she hungry? Is she teething?"

"Is she lactose intolerant?"

"Maybe she's sick, constipated, gassy, congested, scared?"

When I'd assure them that we addressed all of these possibilities, they'd cease asking questions and begin stating what they believed to be truth.

"The room is too dark."

"Her pajamas are itchy."

"It's cancer."

"The room is not dark enough."

"She's thirsty."

"She's autistic."

"She's overtired."

Eventually, I'd nod and smile and agree with them.

"Oh yes," I'd say. "You must be right. I hadn't thought of that." But I know my daughter, and I know the truth. She wasn't any of that. She was simply The Night Fury.

One of the difficulties in dealing with a Night Fury is walking the line between hypochondria and ignoring a valid medical concern. When Mike was about a year old in Sitka, Alaska, his parents began thinking of him as colicky or fussy.

"He just wouldn't sleep," my mother-in-law said. "You'd hold him, and he'd be fine, but the second you'd lay him down, he'd scream his head off."

At eighteen months, his parents began to suspect something

medically wrong. Around the same time, he pointed to his belly and said, "Owie." They took him to Sitka General Hospital, where the doctors said that there was definitely something wrong and that they would need to do exploratory surgery. Few things are as terrifying to a parent as the prospect of exploratory surgery on a baby. My in-laws said no, they would fly to Seattle to a larger, more reputable hospital.

"If you do that," the doctor said, "he won't make the flight."

The matter was put to rest. With no other option, my in-laws relented. He immediately went into surgery. The doctors opened him up to see if they could identify a problem and found that his appendix had burst.

My husband was scarred by this on many levels, including a fair amount of tissue damage on his belly, which he tells our daughters is the result of a great battle he had with a ferocious bear, or sometimes a shark. As a result, it took us a while to accept the fact that sometimes crying is just for the sake of crying, and a tantrum is often just a tantrum.

The most convincing evidence that Ivy's distress was not from any physical ailment was that The Night Fury and accompanying tantrums only surfaced with us. With relatives, babysitters, and random homeless people off the street, she was a delightful child who could easily be rocked to sleep like any other. *Maybe she's allergic to her own parents*, I thought. *Or maybe she just hates us. Already.*

Ivy's comfort when going to sleep was a typical one, a favorite blankie. It could be stiff with snot and drool, and still she'd bury her face in it and say lovingly, "Blankie!" The challenge was getting it away from her for long enough to wash it.

Emilia never latched on to the typical comforts of dolls or

blankets or teddy bears. Her biggest comfort, from the time she first discovered it, has been her belly button. For a solid year and a half, she functioned with a finger permanently placed in her belly button.

There were times when we tried to break her of this, for fear that it would become irritated and cause her pain. Putting her in dresses was difficult, because having her finger in her belly button required that her dress be hiked up around her waist in the front, which sort of defeats the purpose of wearing a nice dress.

She grew out of the habit, for the most part, unless she's feeling anxious, in which case she discreetly seeks it out again. I don't mind this at all; of all the places kids stick their fingers, the belly button isn't that bad.

I tried to coax *Ivy's* finger into her own belly button on occasion, hoping that maybe this method of self-soothing runs in the family. I had visions of The Night Fury placing her finger in her belly button and falling instantly into a deep and contented sleep, but no such luck. For three years we did battle with The Fury, until it dissipated and we found ourselves with a shockingly pleasant child who slept through the night. Those three years were hard, thirty-six months of severe sleep deprivation. Maybe we should have tried the whiskey.

* * *

CHAPTER 17

This Little Piggy Went to the Liquor Store

A s the fury of The Night Fury lessened over time, I found that singing to her could sometimes take the place of speed walk/bouncing. The first few times I sang to my children, the only songs I could think of were from my teenage summer employment at a children's theater camp. I began with "By My Side" from *Godspell*. While this is a beautiful song when sung by someone other than me, the tune is haunting and melancholy.

I searched my brain for something else and came up with a few lines from *Joseph and the Amazing Technicolor Dreamcoat*. These included the phrases: "Hate me and laugh at me" and "Darken my daytime and torture my night." There was another line somewhere in there that went, "Keep those I love from me."

I sang this a few times before realizing that this was far worse than "By My Side," and I was dooming my daughters to a lifetime of depression. I was determined to come up with something more suitable for children, but nothing about smallpox or village starvation or a baby's cradle falling from a tree. I finally settled on a nursery rhyme and ended up filling in verses when I didn't know the words. I sang this to Ivy nightly:

Hush little baby, don't say a word
Mama's gonna buy you a mockingbird
And if that mockingbird don't sing
Mama's gonna buy you a diamond ring
And if that diamond ring don't shine
Mama's gonna drink another bottle of wine

It's interesting that I didn't sing about drinking a bottle of wine, but rather about *another* bottle of wine. Depending on how our finances were doing at the time, it might also have been accurate to substitute the word "box" for "bottle."

And if that bottle of wine goes bad
Mama's gonna ask for help from Dad

But seriously, I don't think a bottle of wine ever had an opportunity to "go bad" in my presence.

And if that dear old dad spaces out
Mama's gonna stomp and scream and shout

Mike has a tendency to space out, as is common with Turners. This complete loss of brain function often occurred when I asked for help. If I got to the point that I asked for help, my bitch-factor was probably already quite high. It's a perfect storm. I would like to note that I do not actually stomp and scream. I have been known to shout.

And if that shouting goes unheard

Another illogical line. If I shout, it is heard.

Mama's gonna buy you a mockingbird

I should also note that this is a lie. I will never buy my children a bird, as I find them dirty and annoying and not meant for either cages or houses. Even if I did buy a bird, it certainly wouldn't be one that would mock me.

Then I'd be full circle and sing the same verses again, as many times as needed to appease The Fury.

* * *

While potty-training, Emilia changed the last line of every song accordingly, much like her uncle Virgil incorporating "ass" into pop music.

She'd walk around the house singing:

We're not too big and we're not too tough
But we use the potty all by ourselves

She altered classics, as well:

Twinkle, twinkle, little star
I use the potty just like a big girl

Rhyme scheme and meter were irrelevant:

Now I know my A-B-Cs
Next time won't you put the poo poo and the pee pee in the
potty and we wear underpants

With age, Emilia's songs took on new originality and could no longer be related back to existing tunes. Her melodies became organic. One of my favorites:

Mama, I love you
All the time, all the time, all the time
All . . . the . . . TIME!

I want a video of this to watch repeatedly during her teenage years.

* * *

Both of my children loved to "play piggies." But let's be honest, *This little piggy had roast beef*? That's ridiculous. And why doesn't the third piggy share with the fourth piggy? Where did the roast beef come from? Did the first piggy buy it at the market? Do pigs even eat beef? That seems odd, as when you picture a farm, cows and pigs are often in close proximity to one another. What exactly happened to the fifth piggy to cause him to run home crying? Did a trauma occur? There are so many loose ends with this rhyme (which fails to rhyme) that I've come up with my own version, one that I feel is more appropriate.

This little piggy went to the toy store
This little piggy gave a wink
This little piggy went to the liquor store
This little piggy sat down to think
And this little piggy cried "More, more, more, more!
I need another drink!"

Sure, it's inappropriate, but so is a lot of great children's literature. Many children's books make me wonder if the authors were high when they wrote. One of my favorite books as a child was Maurice Sendak's *In the Night Kitchen*. And not just because the illustrations included Mickey's tiny penis, which was a strange and intriguing element. The book was banned, of course, so that children wouldn't see a drawing of a boy's penis and become corrupted by it. I can attest to the fact that, of all the bad behavior in my life, of all of the debauchery and sin and other fun I've had, not a smidge of my heathen self turned out the way that it did because I saw Sendak's drawings of little Mickey's penis. I also figured the drawings were not representative of reality. I saw Mickey's nudity the same way I saw Sendak's wild things in *Where the Wild Things Are*, as pure fantasy because surely naked boys didn't have dangly bits. I didn't know what a penis looked like, but I was pretty sure it didn't look like *that*.

Am I the only child who was raised with this?

Ladybug, ladybug, fly away home
Your house is on fire and your children are burning

That can't be right, can it? First of all, it's clunky and doesn't even come close to rhyming. And as far as content, I'm not sure how I feel about the burning children. What if we changed it to: *Your house is under water and your children are drowning*?

No, wait, that's not much better.

Was this an attempt to keep children from playing with matches? Or maybe this is a tool we've developed for kids to assuage any guilt over squashing bugs, as in: That bug's life was so horrific that I really did it a favor by plucking its wings off and grinding it into the pavement.

My stepbrother and I visited our fair share of torture on insects when we were children, though I'm going to go ahead and assert that it was always his idea. It's just one of those things that boys tend to enjoy more than girls. They're simply more barbaric. I preferred games like Serial Killer or Let's Convince Our Parents We're Dead. Why mess around with bugs when we could be playing Car Wreck, which involved collecting rotten cherries from under the cherry tree and smearing them over our bodies while splaying ourselves across the hood of a parent's vehicle?

My stepbrother didn't just squash bugs, though. He sought out butterflies and moths and nailed them to little crosses he'd made in Sunday school. I like to reflect on our enactments not with morbid concern, but with regard for our ingenuity, theatricality, and a religious nod.

I saw the gender differences toward bugs when Emilia and Ivy played with the neighborhood boys their age. When spotting a speck of dirt, my girls would squeal and run to the nearest adult: "It's a bug, and it's going to *get* me!"

The boys sought out insects, smeared them unceremoniously into the sidewalk, and laughed maniacally: "Ha ha ha, you are really truly super *dead*!"

Maybe a rhyme about a ladybug's children burning isn't so far-fetched, after all.

Peter-Peter Pumpkin Eater sounds like an abusive son of a bitch, and I'd like to know if there is any possible silver lining that I can offer my kids regarding Humpty Dumpty. The breaking of an egg is irreversible. The finality of Humpty's condition makes me question if this is actually a nursery rhyme or a lesson on the permanence of death. I also suspect that Humpty didn't fall, he jumped. If I was blindingly pale with an unfortunately bulbous lower half *and* my name had the words "hump" and "dump" in it, I'd probably look for an exit.

If the main characters of a nursery rhyme somehow manage to survive the treacherous plot, they're likely to end up maimed. Jack and Jill didn't fare too well, though at least this rhyme has been tempered somewhat from its origin, which relates to the beheadings of King Louis XVI and Queen Marie Antoinette. And someone should have just put the Three Blind Mice out of their misery. The poor things are blind to begin with, and then that farmer's wife bitch cuts their tails off with a carving knife. I was thinking that maybe she could keep Little Jack Horner in line. He obviously needs some discipline if he thinks he's a good boy for sticking his grubby little hands in the pie. I thought that in Jack Horner, I'd at least identified a nursery rhyme that didn't originate with someone's horrible demise, but I looked it up and this is not so, unless you can overlook a mild case of being hanged, drawn, and quartered. Thank goodness for Dr. Seuss.

* * *

CHAPTER 18

Have Baby, Will Travel

Before children, we traveled to Italy, where my biggest concern was getting Mike to turn off the television. I thought I could accomplish this by trying on some ridiculously expensive lingerie I'd bought. My goal was not to spend our retirement on lingerie, but it was one of those instances when you shop without learning the price until your credit card has been swiped, and then you're too embarrassed to say, "I'm sorry, but I'm just now realizing that I can't afford these panties, after all."

No matter how expensive my lingerie, I was destined for failure when competing with late-night Italian television. I watched one commercial where a woman giggled mischievously as the top button of her blouse popped off under the pressure of her bulging bosom. This advertisement was selling toothbrushes. For a while, I tried to make a connection, but I soon learned it was a waste of time.

Then there were the soft-porn channels. I thought it was recycled eighties porn (big hair is always a tip-off), but now that

I think about it, styles from the eighties were making a comeback at the time, so who knows? I am not as knowledgeable about pornography as . . . people who are knowledgeable about pornography. Anyway, Mike graciously kept changing the channel but then stumbled upon something with which I knew I could not compete. *Conan the Barbarian*. This is one of Mike's all-time favorite movies, for many of the same reasons why I like *Killer Clowns from Outer Space* and *Cannibal Women of the Avocado Jungle of Death*, and though he'd seen it a million times before, he'd never seen it dubbed in Italian. I was not so cruel as to begrudge him such a rare and special opportunity. Besides, at least it was a break from breasts, the power of which we women should use to our advantage to band together and take over the world. I seriously don't think it would be that difficult.

Travel with babies did not involve anything as adventurous as Europe, more often a destination where other family resided so that they could help us wrangle our wee ones. And any television we watched, whether at home or abroad, was animated, rated G, and our entire family could act out every miggot of it. And lingerie? Need I even elaborate?

Our first trip with both children was to Mexico. The flight attendant rattled off her spiel about safety procedures, her toothy smile plastered firmly. I cuddled Ivy in my lap, trying to keep the peace, while Mike and Emilia followed along on the safety card in the row behind me.

"And look!" Mike said. "When the plane lands in the water, it turns into a boat!"

"Ooh! A boat!" Emilia yelled.

"Yes," Mike continued, "and here you can see all the happy people bobbing in the water."

"Swimming!" she screamed.

The flight attendant responded with a dramatic increase in volume, ". . . may be used for GROUP FLOTATION . . ."

Group flotation. Interesting combination of words. Who writes this stuff? All I could think of was Anthony Hopkins as Captain Bligh, yelling at a scruffy, malnourished teen for bitching about his portion of mystery meat. It makes sense that they'd be divvying up a fish, but I always thought of it as seagull.

"We have to pat, Emilia, to help the plane take off," Mike instructed.

At this, Emilia began patting her lap and chanting, "Pat, pat, pat, pat, pat." This made perfect sense to me, as I'd seen more episodes of *Little Einsteins* than the recommended dose. They pat to give their friend Rocket power to take off. Of course.

"Now raise your arms," they said in unison, "as high as you can, and say 'blast off.' BLAST OFF! Now hold on tight 'cause here we go!"

Ivy worked dutifully at her pacifier. An illuminated sign hovered above us. It appeared to represent a man, a woman, a sink, and a television, all with a diagonal line through it, the universal sign of *No!* I deduced that the message was: No men and women permitted watching television in the bathroom at the same time! The threat level must have been high.

When the plane landed, we exited into the chaos that is LAX. After forty-five minutes, we determined that LAX does not have a play area, because logic is not permitted in any of the terminals. Our screaming children convinced us to pay seventy dollars for one hour of admission to the Alaska Airlines Board Room. I wouldn't have done this if there had been one square inch of space available anywhere else in the terminal, but they were fresh out, and in the middle of thousands of crushing bodies, I panicked.

The Board Room comes with complimentary alcohol, and Mike and I abandoned all pretense of caring what others thought of us as parents. With Ivy sleeping and Emilia corralled in front of a portable DVD player, a bloody Mary seemed entirely appropriate.

Hours later, we arrived in Todos Santos, which is a fantastic place to vacation, as long as you can remain easygoing about certain luxuries like running water and electricity. The water periodically shuts off, typically when you *really* need to flush or have soap in your eyes. But if you can survive such minor inconveniences, which you can, then you're guaranteed to have a great trip.

We were excited about vacationing as a newly increased family of four, but does a baby really care about going on vacation? It's not as if she was getting a break from the day job or a needed rest from chores. And a two-year-old doesn't want to go to Mexico; a two-year-old wants brief excitement that can be easily cast aside in favor of a return to routine. The allure of the beach lasted for only a few minutes at a time. Insects devoured her during every sunrise and sunset. Baby scorpions lived in the bathtub.

At least once a day, Emilia reached her arms up, asking to be held, and then buried her face in my neck and said, "Go home? Go home?" She was referring to Boise, and I tried to distract her, bribe her, convince her that this was a vacation for her as much as it was for us.

My in-laws live in Mexico, and Emilia forgave us the torturous ten days of vacation because it allowed her precious time with Nana and Papa. My mother-in-law, as with her interactions with everyone, has limitless energy. She is a two-year-old's dream. And both my children spent a good portion of their infancy asleep on the comfort of their grandfather's chest.

The presence of my in-laws, coupled with the lack of television in our accommodations, presented the perfect opportunity to get our kids away from that addictive little black box. Instead, we found ourselves watching the same movie over and over again, snuggled around the six-inch screen of our portable DVD player. Our intentions were good, but we were destined for failure with opponents like Disney and Pixar.

* * *

Long before children, we joined my in-laws for a camping trip on a beach outside of La Paz, Mexico, with longtime family friends Charlie and Karen. Charlie is one of the toughest men I know. His official day job is commercial fishing in Alaska. If you're ever stranded at sea, Charlie is the guy you want to be stranded with. His countenance reassures. When the fishing season ends, he escapes south with his wife.

When we first arrived, each couple found their own private spot of beach and set up camp. Charlie and Karen, by far the most efficient of the duos present, finished their camp and then began working on the kitchen area and fire pit that would make up the sit-around-the-fire-and-get-drunk-each-night plot of sand.

After laying the bones of the fire pit, Charlie constructed a fire, an art in which all Alaskans are well-versed. With no warning, he suddenly felt a sting in his groin.

"Agh!" The rest of us were otherwise occupied and out of sight, so Charlie dropped his pants and searched for a culprit. After shaking out his clothes, he tentatively put the pants back on and returned to making camp.

The pain hit again.

"Shit!" Sand flew as Charlie again disrobed.

After another thorough investigation of the clothing, Charlie donned his pants.

One leg.

Two legs.

Zipper.

Testicles on fire.

He dropped to the beach, flailing, inhaling sand, and screamed, "What the fuck?!"

The unflappable Charlie lost his cool and succumbed to panic. He removed his pants and underwear and called to his wife.

"Karen?"

Karen, who, like the rest of us, had been unaware of the mounting drama, was busy setting up a makeshift kitchen. With spatula in hand, she walked toward the fire pit to see her husband standing on the beach, naked from the waist down. She misread the distress on his face for pleading.

"Now?" she said. "We haven't even unpacked our sleeping bags yet."

In a state of genital angst, sex was as far removed from Charlie's conscious thought as possible.

"Something is biting me. I need your help."

"Oh. Are you okay?"

"No," he answered.

Karen examined the pants. Any sign of bug or beast eluded her.

"Go ahead, put your pants back on," Karen said.

"I don't want to."

"Charlie, it's fine. Come on, the Turners are going to see and never go camping with us again."

Charlie looked at his wife warily and then again examined the clothes.

"I promise you," Karen assured him, "it's gone. Whatever it was, it's gone. Now hurry up and put your pants back on."

It was as he expected.

One leg.

Two legs.

Zipper.

Testicles on fire.

"Fuuuucckkkk!"

"Oh! I see it!" Karen exclaimed. "Look, Charlie, I see it!" A fair-sized scorpion scuttled away from the scene. Charlie, cupping his genitals with his left hand, ripped the spatula from Karen's grasp with his right and pounded the scorpion until it disintegrated into prehistoric sections of its former self. The two stood in silence for a moment.

"Jesus," Karen said, "what do we do?"

"I don't know," Charlie answered.

He figured he'd better just sit down, smoke a joint, and prepare to die, not knowing that the creature was relatively harmless, though he wouldn't have described it as such, in light of its injurious attitude toward his genitals.

Mike and I showed up, because by that time Mike had set up the tent and I'd had sufficient time to complain about the fact that there was sand everywhere.

"Honey," Mike said as we walked toward the fire pit, "we're camping on a beach."

"I know," I said, "but it's just so *sandy*."

"Whoa," Mike said as we reached Charlie and Karen. "Are we interrupting something?"

They filled us in on the backstory and Charlie graciously donned his clothing, though his fear was palpable. My mother-in-law joined us. Charlie sat, emasculated, as Karen relayed the story yet again.

While Charlie had been repeatedly removing and donning his pants, my father-in-law wandered among the dunes with a shovel, looking for a suitable spot in which to relieve himself. He came across a makeshift toilet left by a predecessor. A deep hole had been dug in the ground, over which sat a genuine toilet seat. These constructs hide in the dunes of Mexico's beaches, created by the local fishermen who make camp there.

Pleased with his find, he sat down to do his business, discovering midway through, by means of a terrible sting on the tip of his penis, that the hole was inhabited by a family of hornets. In great pain, he attempted to run, pants down around his ankles, from the hornets, but the worst of the damage was done. Apparently, hornets don't mind living *in* a shit hole, but they don't necessarily want to be shit *on*.

Frantic, my father-in-law ran back to camp, pants still down around his ankles. He wanted help, with no clear idea of what had actually happened and what help would entail, but he didn't necessarily want to be seen. He also hadn't completed his initial mission of relieving himself. The pain crushed all ongoing mental dilemmas, and he ran screaming into camp. No one heard him at first, as we were all saying our farewells to Charlie, who fully expected to keel over at any moment.

"Shit! Shit! Help!" my father-in-law cried. He reached camp and stopped short, struck into silence by the sight of Charlie, who sat, surrounded by the rest of us, delicately cupping his crotch.

"A scorpion stung me in the groin," Charlie explained.

"A hornet stung the end of my penis," my father-in-law countered.

"Touché," said Charlie, who was slowly accepting the fact that he wasn't going to die, after all.

Mike was in the midst of an intense moral dilemma. He is one of those people who has taken various forms of survival training and medical assistance classes in his life. By all accounts, he is a good guy to have around in the event that someone needs first aid of some sort. Yet, confronted with the ailing genitalia of his father and Charlie, he was at a loss.

We lagged at the periphery. The wives of the two men stood in the midst of it all, looking back and forth between their wounded husbands.

My mother-in-law was the first to speak. "Who wants a margarita?"

* * *

Cerritos is one of those beaches that is a little more unfortunate every time you visit. Ten years ago, it was sand and water. It's no longer the secret of a privileged few. Now there are waiters, music, trash, dogs, RVs, and resorts. Actually, there were always trash and dogs.

I sat on a blanket, beer to my right and baby in my lap, when a scorpion stung me on the buttock. My father-in-law swears that I levitated. The sting was less painful than that of a bee—this was just a toddler of a scorpion—but I was desperate to put some distance between the little monster and three-month-old Ivy.

While jumping up and jarring my infant, probably causing more damage than the scorpion would have, I yelled, "A scorpion just stung me on the butt! A scorpion just stung me on the butt!" Three of the men in the group descended on the little beast with furious flip-flops, taking turns pounding the thing until it curled up into a sad and dead little speck.

We had other encounters with the creatures whose world we'd invaded, including mice, cockroaches, ants, earwigs, a variety of lizards, and the occasional bat. Mexico overflows with little crawlers just waiting to scare you, bite you, sting you, or suck your blood. During my last trip, a vacationer got hit by a sting ray, the barb neatly lancing her toe. Sting rays are known to inflict incredible pain. Her only consolation was that she received excellent medical care for a total cost of twenty-five dollars.

Completely harmless, but high on the *ick* factor are the cockroaches, the frequent killing of which loudly punctuated every night. Big juicy ones that crackle and crunch when you get them, so you half hope you miss. It's best just to not get up in the middle of the night at all, but that's impossible with two children. So you grab a book, and the loud slap of it on the concrete floor scares the crap out of your sleeping and unsuspecting spouse.

* * *

Emilia and I walked behind our rented house in Todos Santos to the passion fruit cemetery. We'd play catch with the decaying little orbs, littering the ground in shades of green, yellow, and finally, brown. This was the sort of catch that spans distances of only a foot; after all, she was two at the time. When she decided she was finished with catch, she turned to walk back to the house and said, "That's my castle." I smiled. But then, once inside, she again asked to go home.

Twenty-four hours later, we landed at LAX. Emilia thoroughly enjoyed deplaning via bus. Customs was easy, though the other passengers shot us snide looks when we were escorted to the front of the line ahead of all the childless travelers. After customs, we were directed to a special elevator that would accommodate our behemoth stroller and provide a shortcut to the next security check. After getting off the elevator, we got in the next line, taking our place behind thirty or forty people. Our children had entirely wilted, but despite their screaming, no one offered to bump us up. LAX was fresh out of special treatment.

After security, we ran harder, Mike pushing the mammoth stroller, the girls smiling as if on a roller coaster. My T-shirt was soaked through with sweat, not in a sexy way, but in an offensively odorous sort of way. An assortment of carry-on luggage draped my arms.

"Once again, paging Turner, party of four, paging Turner party of four. This is your *final* boarding call; please report to Gate 33 for *immediate* departure." This guy was doing very little to disguise the annoyance in his voice. You would think that two hours would be enough of a layover, but not so.

We made it and settled into our seats, Mike and Emilia in a row across the aisle, Ivy enjoying the comforts of her pacifier in my lap. I wouldn't have enough room to put the tray table down, but that wouldn't stop me from ordering a glass of wine when the time came. I've perfected a balancing act of sorts to enjoy wine in such situations without spilling it or waking a sleeping baby, or doing both at once. If you wake a baby by spilling wine *on* her, you are immediately out of the running for Mother of the Year.

"Daddy, read the boat story!" Emilia demanded, shoving the emergency procedure pamphlet at Mike. He did so, weaving tales of magical planes that morph into boats.

"And all the passengers are so happy because they get to go swimming!"

"Yay, swimming! We go swimming at the *beach* and the *water* and the *ocean*, Daddy."

"Yes, and then they live happily ever after," he concluded.

They began their enthusiastic patting and chanting to help the plane take off.

"BLAST OFF!"

"Good job, Emilia," Mike said. "Now we're going to go home. Do you want to go home?"

I stole a moment of closed eyes and thought of "home." It was a world I'd never anticipated, accessorized with Diaper Genies, Otter Pops, and Dr. Seuss. It included a liquor cabinet, but still, I was a long way from secret agent.

Emilia had wanted nothing more than *home* the entire trip. She was grubby, tired, and had spent the day surviving on Cheetos, lollipops, and other junk. She looked up at her father and smiled sweetly before speaking. "No." She yawned. "No go home."

* * *

CHAPTER 19

Living the Dream

I woke at seven on the couch, two-year-old Ivy sprawled across my belly. She was a sleeping, sweaty mass. Mike and I had spent the night lying awake in bed, listening to her pleading and pounding on the door. That's what we were reduced to: Locking her in her room, pledging not to open her door between the hours of 10 p.m. and 6 a.m. The only exception to that rule was if we detected the distinct odor of poo.

Putting her to bed slowly got easier, but the middle of the night was still treacherous. She'd woken at 1 a.m., and the Fury took over and lasted for three hours. It began with crying, which turned into pleading for Mommy and Daddy, and ended with "Watch *Scooby-Doo*! Watch *Scooby-Doo*!" until she'd finally fallen back to sleep. She started crying again at 5 a.m. I'd remained still and gritted my teeth until the clock read 6:00. That was the glorious hour when I was thankful the night was over. I retrieved her, we adjourned to the couch, and she fell asleep on me without another tear.

I woke at seven not because Ivy stirred, but because my father-in-law, visiting for a few days, approached. He was quiet coming up the steps from the finished basement where he slept, but he wrestled with the baby gate at the top of the stairs.

"Damn gate!"

He didn't see us on the couch.

"Ivy's asleep," I whispered, but he didn't hear me.

"Stupid contraption!" He shook it as if to loosen all of the screws so that it might disassemble at his feet.

"Hey, we're on the couch over here."

"Stupid thing is *broken*!"

Ivy was already waking, so I figured I might as well help him. I stood and walked to open the gate; he saw me.

"Oh, sorry," he whispered.

He attempted to shut the gate behind him but left it half-latched. I made a mental note to lock it when he wasn't looking. We walked to the kitchen, and he smiled at Ivy, slit-eyed and half asleep on my shoulder.

"No!" She glared at him. "*My* mommy!"

"Why are you two out here?" he asked. "Did she not sleep well?"

"She was screaming most of the night." I yawned.

"Funny," he said, "I didn't hear anything."

"Well, you're pretty much deaf," I commented.

"What?" he asked.

I dropped it.

"Are you feeling better?" I asked. The night before, he'd complained of a sinus headache.

"Yes," he said. "I think that stuff you gave me really helped."

"The Claritin?"

"Either that or the euthanasia," he said.

"The *what*?"

"Oh, whatever it's called. Euthanasia? Echinacea?"

I was dying to highlight the differences between mercy killing and the herbaceous flowering plant of the daisy family, but I bit my tongue.

"I'm glad you're feeling better," I said, and I was. "I'm going to get this family moving. Got to get these kids to school." By school I meant day care, but calling it school made me feel better.

The next hour was a flurry of giggles and tears, pajamas and dresses, tooth-brushing and potty-training. Meltdowns accompanied every action.

"Let's get in the car, girls." I tried to lift Ivy into her seat.

"No! *My* do it!"

Emilia added encouragement as Ivy spent five minutes trying to crawl into the car seat. "You can do it, Mivy!" *Mivy* meant *my Ivy* and is how Emilia referred to her sister.

After ten excruciating minutes, I had both children in their seats and buckled.

"Good job, Mivy, you did it," Emilia said.

"No, *my* mommy!" Ivy said.

We arrived at day care, where a little boy, whose name I didn't know, told Emilia he loved her. She said she loved him back. She gave me a kiss and a hug, and then was off with her fellow four-year-olds.

Ivy's class of two-year-olds was more chaotic and less lovey-dovey. Snot and tantrums abounded. She didn't want to be released from me, and I didn't blame her. I sat with her in a chair in the corner, in a silent snuggle. Miss Pam put breakfast on the table, and the other children gathered.

"Ivy," she called. "Do you want to have breakfast?"

"No," Ivy answered. "*My* mommy."

"We're having pancakes with syrup for breakfast."

"Bye-bye, Mommy." She launched herself from my arms.

I walked to my car with the potential of a child-free day before me and only the slightest shadow of guilt.

* * *

"Mom, I'm going to Africa," Emilia said. We're on our way home.

"Oh, okay," I answered.

"Miss Dottie, when my teeth fall out the tooth fairy will turn them into gold and give me a special present and I'll get big teeth just like you! It's going to be so much fun! I'm so excited!"

"That's great, honey," I said. "But you just called me Miss Dottie."

"Oh." She giggled. "That's silly!"

She'd call me Miss Dottie half a dozen times throughout the evening. Some parents would be troubled by this, but I was not.

"Mommy? Dinner?" Ivy asked.

"We'll have dinner when we get home, Ivy."

"Dinner!" she demanded.

"Yes, Ivy. I'll make you dinner as soon as we get home."

"*Dinner!*"

She was angered by the fact that I couldn't produce dinner right there in the car.

"Mivy," Emilia said. "Mommy's driving the car, but we'll have dinner when we get home."

"No, *my* mommy!"

My father-in-law commanded the kitchen. He made burgers with venison from a recent hunt in Alaska. I was squeamish about this but did my best to hide it. Stray bits of raw meat covered the counters. I appeased the kids with an assortment of kid food.

Mike's sister, Sandi, arrived with her husband, Matt, and my nieces, Bella and Rosie. Bella rushed me with a hug. Rosie was so excited about things she wanted to share from her day that she could barely breathe. Sandi was stylish in clothes I could never wear. Matt is the family's best bartender. He and I conducted an entire conversation with facial expressions. It went like this:

Matt: Do you want a drink?

Me: Yes.

Matt: Margarita?

Me: Yes.

Matt: Strong?

Me: Yes.

"So, Dad," Sandi said. "I bet you're eager to get back to Mom in Alaska." Though they live in Mexico, they still spend summers in Sitka. Business had temporarily taken them in different directions, but they'd only been apart for a few days.

"Yes," he said. "I definitely need some *alone* time with my wife."

"Ew," said Mike.

"Too much info," agreed Sandi.

Matt handed me the perfect beverage. The girls built a fort in the living room.

"Shaka-khan, your mom!" Virgil arrived, a tsunami flooding the kitchen.

"Shaka-khan, *your* mom," Mike countered.

"You know," I interjected, "you guys have the same mom."

They ignored me.

"What are you up to?" Mike asked.

"I'm going camping this week," answered Virgil. "It's up past Lucky Peak. There's a sign for Twin Springs, population two. Although now it's really one because the guy's wife died."

No one had any idea what he was talking about.

"How's work?" Mike asked.

"Fucking awesome," Virgil said. "I'm doing tile now. I fucking hate tile, but I'm really good at it. My boss said, 'Virgil, I know you don't like to do tile, but just do the tile. Do your hyper-freak-out-shit, then just do the job.' So that's what I do. You guys got any tequila?"

The room ignored this inquiry. It was a weeknight, and we questioned if we had the collective stamina to endure an evening of Virgil plus tequila. Matt handed him a beer.

"I have a new roommate," he continued. "She's sixty and four foot ten, but she wears high heels all the time and she's fucking hot."

"Virgil," Sandi interrupted, "*language*." She looked toward the living room, where the girls nestled in their not-quite-soundproof fort.

"Oh, sorry," he said. "So my new roommate has flowers and old-lady knickknack shit all over the house. I don't even know where to fucking sit. She even has these little stairs that lead up to her bed. She's fucking awesome."

"Who is this?" my father-in-law asked. "A new girlfriend?"

"No, Dad! Ew, gross. She's sixty, but she's hot as hell. So my buddy Dustin got punched in the nose last night. Or maybe it was a head butt. I don't know, all I know is I see blood coming out of my buddy's nose, so we chase down this guy and we've got him cornered and he's shirtless and scared shitless and there's like twelve of us ready to pounce on this guy like a *puma*. Like a fucking . . . *puma*. Is the food ready? I'm starving!"

The food was ready, and the rest of the story was never told or didn't exist. The burgers were fantastic and beat into submission my squeamishness about venison.

The girls graced us with a fashion show, a combination of rain boots, princess dresses, and hats made out of paper. The evening progressed with a mixture of alcohol and family and parenting that a younger me couldn't have conceived. Not just my teenage self, but also the thirty-year-old me, just five years prior.

We called my mother-in-law in Alaska and passed the phone around. Her presence was missed.

"Well, I confess that I'm having a martini right now. Actually, it's my second martini," she said.

"I'm on my third margarita," I conceded.

"I think I'm going to stop at two," she said. "There's a bear in the backyard."

"Holy shit. What do you do in that situation? Call 9-1-1?" I asked.

"Oh, no. It's just a bear. That's Alaska for you. I'm sure it'll be on its way soon."

"You're so badass," I said.

"The dog has to pee, but I'm not letting him out. I'd rather he pee on the floor than get eaten."

"Well, you're missed here, but we'll look forward to seeing you in a few weeks," I said. "Your husband is dying to talk to you, so I'll pass the phone to him now."

We said our goodbyes, and I handed the phone to my father-in-law, who'd been clawing at me for his turn to speak with his wife.

"No talking dirty," I warned.

He grabbed the phone from me with a defiant smirk. He told her about the burgers he made, and she told him about the bear. They'd been married for more than forty years but still caused each other to blush.

Sandi bathed the girls in shifts. Virgil cleaned the kitchen with vigor. Matt and Mike planned a mountain-biking trip, the focus of which seemed to be the beer they'd drink after. I packed the next day's lunches.

Life wasn't perfect, and I knew it never would be. The immediate future was another sleepless night, but we'd made it through the day without any children injuring themselves and without any adults soiling themselves. The kids were happy, their parents had drinks, and those drinks were all half-full.

* * *

Sneak Peek of

Mommy Had a Little Flask

CHAPTER 1

The Vice Squad

"Shaka-kahn, your mom!" Virgil stormed the kitchen. My brother-in-law is incapable of entering a house quietly. He has no knowledge of the custom of knocking, and he disregards typical greetings of "hello" or "hi, how are you?" in favor of his own salutation of "Shaka-kahn, your mom."

"Shaka-kahn, *your* mom," my husband, Mike, replied.

"You know," I said for the hundredth time, "you guys have the same mom." They ignored me.

"So, I got this new job," Virgil said.

"Lord, help us," muttered Mike, handing his brother a beer. Virgil is perpetually on the brink of losing a job, landing a job, getting a raise, or not getting paid. This latter event is a curious one to which only Virgil is prone. When he needs cash, it's not because he spent his money at a dive bar or got fired or failed to show up for work, it's because a boss inexplicably failed to pay him.

"And I mean, thank God I got fired from my old one," Virgil

continued. As he spoke, he lifted up his shirt and caressed his large, hairy belly with both hands. "Well, I didn't really get fired, I quit, but that's great because my new job is awesome and comes with a huge raise. It's like crazy because there are these two other guys, but they don't know what the hell they're doing, and now I'm their supervisor. I just started today. Amanda, what's that smell?" This was the first time he addressed me directly, and I had a sudden flash of paranoia that all odors in my home were attributed solely to me.

"Jalapeños," I answered. "They'll be ready in five minutes." I'd been cultivating an addiction to stuffed jalapeños, which I justified because they are technically a vegetable. While I may stuff them with meat and cheese, they are still a *vegetable* stuffed with meat and cheese. My rationale is based on an important parenting technique that I like to call Willful Denial of Fact. It's the same logic I employ when telling myself that my kids eat healthily because I put cucumber slices on their plates, never mind the fact that they don't touch the cucumbers and only consume foods in the shapes of fish and dinosaurs. Willful Denial of Fact has other uses, as well. For instance, you can't tell me that I consumed an entire bottle of wine myself if the wine came out of a box.

"Virgil?" I asked. "Is it possible for you not to rub your big, furry stomach in my kitchen? It's a bit . . . distracting." I wanted to say "gross" but was trying to be kind. He mercifully lowered his shirt but continued running both hands over his middle.

"What's the new job?" Mike asked.

"I don't know, like cleaning up trash in an old crappy house, and then we'll rehab it. I'll start on Monday."

"I thought you said you started today," Mike said.

"No." Virgil shook his potbelly for emphasis, a signature move. "Do you even hear anything anyone else says? I said I'll start on *Monday*. Did you guys hear about the dude that got caught with the thing in his car?"

"What are you talking about?" I couldn't recall seeing a headline about a "dude" and his "thing."

"At least he didn't kill a monkey," he said. "*That* guy really screwed up. I mean, what kind of sick bastard kills a monkey?"

At the time, Boise held a collective anger toward a yet-to-be-identified monkey killer. Someone broke into the Boise Zoo, was spotted by security but then evaded the police, and after all was said and done, a monkey was dead. Eventually the monkey killer would be arrested, and it turned out his aim was not to injure a monkey, but instead to *steal* a monkey. Perhaps he held an obsession with David Schwimmer's character on *Friends* and wanted a little Marcel of his own. As disturbing as his intention to steal the unfortunate creature was, the fact that he made it into the zoo at 4 a.m. and then into the monkey enclosure was even more troubling. Aren't the animal exhibits locked somehow? If an idiot who thinks that he can keep a stolen monkey as his pet can get into the cage, then surely a monkey, no doubt smarter than the aforementioned idiot, can get out. In any case, while attempting to remove the monkey from the zoo, the man got bit on the hand. Apparently monkeys don't like to be kidnapped and wrapped in people's coats. Especially by drunk people, which this idiot was. In response, the man beat the monkey on the head with a branch, and the monkey later died. Virgil's comment about the monkey was one of those rare instances when he says something completely off the wall, but I actually know what he's talking about.

"Let's not talk about the *demise* of the *primate*," I said, coding my language so that my daughters in the next room wouldn't overhear. We were frequent patrons of the zoo, and I wasn't yet ready to break the news. I'd also been (poorly) fielding many questions of late from my five-year-old, Emilia, about death in general. I was honest about the "Everybody dies" part, but then usually followed it up with "Who wants to go get some ice cream and pick out a new toy!" I wanted to have my thoughts in order and avoid this scenario before we tackled the monkey business. Otherwise, Emilia was likely to become obsessed with death once she figured out that conversations about it resulted in ice-cream cones and Barbie dolls.

"I'm going to smoke," Virgil said.

"No cigarette butts on the ground!" I commanded.

"Calm down, woman!" he yelled. "There's no need to yell. I clean up after myself."

I don't like to think of myself as someone who yells often, but in Virgil's case, it's fairly appropriate. Yelling as my primary means of communicating with Virgil has engendered in him an irrational fear of me. This fear, in turn, has resulted in a marked decline in the average number of times he asks me for money. Now he asks Mike for money. The last time he did this, about three months prior, Mike called me, and the conversation was as follows:

Mike (with trepidation): "Amanda, I want to loan my brother some money."

I generally take the view that loaning money to Virgil is not a wise idea. However, Virgil is Mike's brother, and if he wants to loan money to him, I'm not going to interfere or question his decision.

Me: "Okay, what do you want me to do?"

Mike: "The power company won't turn his power back on until someone calls them and pays with a credit card. I'm driving, and I just can't take care of this right now."

This made me feel a little bit better about the situation. I'd rather the money go directly to the power company than to Virgil to take to the power company after a brief stop at a dive bar for a shot and a beer. And a shot and a beer and a beer and a beer.

Me: "I can call for you, but I'm assuming I'll need his account number and address." (Some might think it odd that I do not know Virgil's address or even in what neighborhood he resides, but I'm perfectly comfortable with this lack of information.)

Mike: "Yes, you'll have to get that from him."

Me: "Then why didn't he just call me himself?"

Mike: "I asked him to, but he's afraid of you."

Me: "Okay, that makes sense."

Virgil finished smoking and reentered the kitchen as I took the jalapeños from the oven. Mike's other sibling, Sandi, arrived.

"Chello, everyone," she greeted me and her brothers.

"What's up, Sister Christian," Virgil said.

"Are you actually getting shorter?" Mike asked.

"Let's hope not," she answered. "I don't have a lot to work with here." Sandi is four feet ten inches tall but compensates for her lack of height with endless energy and spunk. "But, you know, I've never really had a problem being short."

"That's good," said Virgil, "since you can't do shit about it."

Sandi ignored him and tried a jalapeño. "Ooh, nummers," she said. "That is some *nums*."

Nummers is one of those absolutely ridiculous fabricated baby-talk words that drive me insane. It's so cutesy and ridiculous that I hear it and find myself wanting to cause some sort of destruction. Like I want to find a flower bed and trample it. I want to take something cute and make it not cute, because that's the reaction I have when a grown person, or anyone over the age of eighteen months, describes something as *nummers*. I think Sandi bears the initial responsibility for creating and using this horrible non-word, which should be universally banned, but other members of the Turner clan have since picked it up. I grit my teeth when anyone says *nummers*, especially in light of the fact that they are usually trying to pay me a compliment. *Did you mean to tell me that what I made was delicious or wonderful or excellent or even just good? Because I will take any of those over the word nummers.* But now, Sandi was creating new forms of what isn't even a word to begin with. Tacking on "that is some nums" was over-the-top unacceptable and a blight on the English language.

Another one that disturbed me, but that Sandi thankfully grew out of, was *wawa* for water. I understand that when a child learns to speak, "water" may come out as sounding more like "wawa." But that is no reason for the parent to then begin referring to water as *wawa*. It is the parent who is supposed to teach the child how to speak. The parent is not supposed to adopt the child's baby talk as the new and improved English. I also cringe at use of the word *binkie* or some other such cutesy and idiotic word for pacifier. It's a pacifier, plain and simple. Sure it's four syllables, but so is procreation. And if you are old enough to procreate and end up with a baby out of the deal, then you are old enough to say "pacifier" and "delicious" and "water."

Maybe when your child is learning to talk and comes up

with the substitute of *wawa* for water, you let it slip once or twice and ask them if they want some *wawa*. The correct course of action is to immediately reprimand yourself and vow never to make such a grievous error again. Not only did Sandi fail to reprimand herself as such when her daughters were tiny, but she continued to use the non-word of *wawa* long past when her children could say "water". Seeing a grown adult ask a six-year-old if she wants *wawa* makes me want to call Child Protective Services.

"Sandi," I said, "I'm sorry, but I absolutely have to put my foot down. *Nummers* is not a word. *Nummers* has never been a word, and now you're bastardizing even that."

"What are you talking about? What did I say?"

"You said, 'That is some *nums*.'"

"So?"

"You just can't do that!"

At this point, my husband and his siblings rolled their eyes. Just as I feel I've spent years dealing with their butchered speech, they feel they've spent years dealing with my bitching about their butchered speech.

"Sure I can," said Sandi. "Why not?"

"Don't pay any attention to her," Virgil said. "It's just because she's a writer. She can't help it. She was born that way." He turned to me then and said, "People are always so amazed when I tell them that your dad is Dean Koontz."

"You tell people what?" I asked.

"Isn't your dad a writer, too? I tell everyone your dad is Dean Koontz. You know, the guy who wrote *The Shining*."

"Wow," I said. "It would be pretty difficult for you to mess up that statement any worse than you just did." Suddenly *nummers* and *wawa* didn't seem so bad.

"Isn't your dad a writer?"

"Yes."

"But your dad isn't Dean Koontz?" He looked perplexed, as if there was one male writer on the earth named Dean Koontz, and he'd written one book called *The Shining*. So if my father was a writer, in Virgil's mind he must be *that* guy.

"I feel like I'm suddenly in *The Twilight Zone*," I groaned.

"Did he write that, too?" Virgil asked excitedly.

"No, and Dean Koontz didn't write *The Shining*."

"But your dad wrote *The Shining*, right?"

"No, Virgil. My dad is not Dean Koontz, nor is my dad Stephen King, who wrote *The Shining*."

"Huh," he said. "Well, that's what I tell people." The way he said this made me think that he didn't have any intention of changing this story in the future. He'd latched on to it as truth, and as far as he was concerned, whenever he discussed his sister-in-law, he would include the little bit about how my dad is Dean Koontz, the guy who wrote *The Shining*.

"These jalapeños would go great with a bloody Mary," Sandi said, opening the cabinet to get bloody Mary makings. "Amanda! Where's the booze?" she gasped. "And why am I seeing Honey Nut Cheerios instead of vodka?"

"Don't panic," I assured her. "I had to relocate the alcohol."

It only took me a few years to figure out that letting children play with liquor bottles is inappropriate. Our kitchen is small. There's only one suitable place to keep the booze, one shelf that will accommodate the tallest of liquor bottles. Unfortunately, this is also the shelf that is easiest accessed by toddlers. They never broke a bottle of booze or even attempted to open one, but they did like to rearrange them. At the age of two, Ivy would remove all of the bottles and carry them one by one over to her *Toy Story* table, where she would line them up over the background of Buzz and Woody's smiling faces. It was a game, a puzzle of sorts, and eventually she'd return them all to their shelf. She liked the pretty bottles, and with me standing there to ensure safety, I didn't have a problem with it. But on occasion, she would do this while wearing nothing but her diaper. This shouldn't matter, of course, but in my mind, her lack of clothing intensified the debauchery. I smiled at the sight of her but also felt an intense fear that a fire would spontaneously break out, causing the police and fire departments to rush into my home before I had a chance to tidy—because, of course, the few minutes I had before they arrived would be spent furiously applying makeup and searching for a more slimming outfit, as opposed to clothing my child or putting away the liquor bottles. They'd see Ivy in her diaper, presiding over rum, tequila, vodka, and perhaps an innocuous mixer like tonic, at which point they'd know that I am a very bad person.

Once this scenario played itself out in my head, I let Ivy play one last game of Liquor Store before moving the booze permanently out of reach. Other parents might think me slow or unfit for not curbing the behavior as soon as it started, but when it comes to positive parenting, I don't often get things right on the first or fourth try. I take baby steps.

"I had to move the liquor bottles out of reach from the kids," I told Sandi. "They're up there now." I pointed to a high cabinet, one that I realized was probably out of Sandi's reach as well.

"So lame," she said, staring wistfully at the cabinet.

"I don't have the goods, in any case," I said.

"That's all right. I just thought I'd swing by. I should probably head home and get some work done."

"Me, too," said Virgil. "I'm out."

"Those jalapeños really were *nummers*," Sandi said to Virgil as they headed for the door.

"Hey, did you hear about that dude that got caught with the thing in his car?"

"Yeah," she answered. "But at least he didn't kill a monkey."

* * *

CHAPTER 2

Duct Tape for Dora

"Are you nervous?" Sandi asked.

This is the worst possible question someone can ask me. I'm instantly fearful that I've forgotten about an upcoming exam or that I have to teach a class on something about which I have no knowledge, like open heart surgery or rocket science. When I realize those scenarios are ridiculous and have no basis in reality, I wonder if I'm due to receive the results of a major biopsy. And if I've forgotten that today's the day the doctor tells me how long I'll live, then I must have Alzheimer's, even though I'm in my mid-thirties. At which point I decide to write my own obituary while I'm still lucid. I don't want anyone else screwing it up.

"Nervous about what?" I asked.

"About kindergarten."

"Why would I be nervous?" I crossed the obituary off my to-do list. "I'm not the one who has to learn to read."

"Yes, but are you nervous about sending Emilia to school?"

"Not at all," I said. "She's been in full-time day care from the start. I think she'll be fine."

"But this is different. This is *kindergarten*."

When Sandi tells me I should be nervous about something, I tend to believe her. She has two daughters with the same age difference as my girls, but her girls are older, so she experiences all the stages of parenthood a few years before I do. The way she said *kindergarten* made my heart tighten in my chest. Were there kindergarten hazing rituals that I didn't know about? Was there some sort of women's self-defense class for five-year-olds that I should enroll her in?

"I don't think Emilia's going to have any problems," I said.

"I agree. Emilia will be just fine. *You* might be a mess, though."

"We'll see."

I put my own emotional well-being to the side and gave some thought to how Emilia would do. Maybe *hazing* wasn't necessarily a worry, but would she be bullied or teased? Such scenarios are far more terrifying than physical playground injuries. Aside from the universal parental fear that another child might be mean to my own, and that I might inappropriately exact revenge on that child's mother by engaging in a catfight at a PTA meeting, I held one other apprehension about the transition to kindergarten: nap time.

Emilia is a sleeper. Leading up to the first day of kindergarten, I tried to eradicate the nap in preparation and asked her day-care teachers for their assistance.

"We tried to keep her up," they'd report at the end of the day, "but she fell asleep anyway, right in the middle of painting." This would be evidenced by a large patch of blue paint in the middle of her forehead. The kid needs sleep. Even at the age of five, she enjoyed a two-hour nap during the day, despite the fact that she slept ten hours every night.

I shouldn't complain about this, as most parents equate the outgrowth of nap time to the death of a loved one. Nap time is a dear friend, that treasured hour or two when parents of small children regain some semblance of sanity. It's a time for parents to nap themselves, put away the dishes, or meet up for a nooner. Most of all, it's a time to steel oneself for the next segment of parenthood that extends from post-nap to bedtime.

Being the accommodating and gracious child that she is, Emilia continued to nap long after others her age stopped. This was a nice balance to Ivy, who cruelly refused to sleep through the night for three torturous years. Before she started kindergarten, we resigned ourselves to the possibilities that Emilia would either be very tired at the end of the day or fall asleep in the middle of class. Both would prove true.

I had no worries about Emilia's ability to handle actual schoolwork, and the introduction of homework into our daily routine excited me. That might sound insane, but when I was in school, I was a nerd and loved homework. I suspected that Emilia would, too. And as far as Mike and I were concerned, homework meant less television, a break from which was welcome. Specifically, we longed for a hiatus from Dora and Diego, not simply because these animated little cousins insist on yelling everything that comes out of their mouths, but also because Dora and Diego had completely failed in teaching our children Spanish. They now think that maps can talk and believe monkeys wear boots, but their Spanish skills are still as limited as my own. I'd been hoping to cultivate little translators, but no such luck.

My mother, known to my children as Grammy, could not understand why I don't like Diego.

"But he's so cool," she said.

"No, he's not. He's obnoxious. He's constantly yelling. Everything has to be at shouting volume, and the animation sucks."

"But he's an animal *rescuer*," she said. "He *rescues animals*." Grammy is an animal lover, and nothing is more appealing to her than the idea of someone who spends his life rescuing animals. Even if that someone is imaginary. "Speaking of animals," she continued, "maybe when they catch the monkey killer and put him on trial, I can fly out, and we can go to the trial together."

"Do they let people do that?" I asked.

"Why not?"

"Well, it's not like going to a concert or an exhibit at a museum."

"And we could take *snacks*," she continued.

"You want to see this guy hang, don't you?"

"He killed a monkey," she answered, which was her way of saying, *You bet your ass, I do.* "And maybe we could take Emilia and Ivy!"

"To a monkey murder trial?"

"They could learn about the justice system."

Grammy's idea was starting to sound like a good one, which was a reminder to myself that I should never be allowed to homeschool my children.

I abandoned this idea, as well as the fantasy of a cartoon making our children bilingual, and enrolled Emilia in a kindergarten class. Not just any kindergarten class. Half the day was taught in Mandarin Chinese. When Mike first brought this program's existence to my attention, I thought it sounded too intense and was worried about the stress it might cause Emilia.

"Are you excited about going to kindergarten?" I asked her.

"Will there be friends there who are this tall?" she countered, placing a flat palm on the top of her head.

"Yes, there will be plenty of other kids who are your age. And your height."

"Then yes, I'm excited."

"And you're going to learn Chinese there," I said.

"Okay. And will they have lunch there?"

"Yes," I assured her. "I promise you will continue to be fed on a regular basis."

If you think about it, telling a child she's going to learn Chinese is no more intimidating than showing her the face of a clock and telling her she's going to learn how to tell time. So Emilia's language exposure went from watching red-eyed tree frogs cry for *ayudame!* to hours of complex Chinese characters.

The elementary school we enrolled Emilia in, by way of lottery and wait-list, a process that reminded me of applying for college, was on the other side of town. Our daughter would spend the first half of the day in English with Ms. Sherod, and in the afternoon, she'd battle fatigue while learning to count in Chinese with Mr. Li. Both Ms. Sherod and Mr. Li are shockingly short, which is fitting for kindergarten teachers, as five-year-olds are low to the ground themselves. Both have an unmistakable knack for dealing with children, but also a firmness that makes it clear who is in charge. The confidence that I felt in Emilia's teachers made driving across town worth it.

I'll also take on a commute so that my children are not subjected to the incompetence of our local crossing guard. An old man sits in a plastic chair at an intersection near my house. When children approach, he is invariably sleeping, his chin resting heavy on his chest, or he's staring off into space. Conversely, when there are no children in sight, he can be found standing in the middle of the intersection, stop sign hanging down by his side, oblivious to the fact that the kids have long since made their way across the street safely, regardless of his ineptitude. I don't have any prejudices against the elderly, but if you reach the age when your faculties are diminished in any way, perhaps it's best not to assume a position in which you are responsible for the safety of children at a busy intersection.

As kindergarten approached, Sandi declared that she and her daughters would take Emilia shopping for a new backpack and lunch box. This shopping event was touted for months and greatly anticipated. The day arrived, and Sandi, along with Emilia's beloved cousins, Bella and Rosie, took Emilia shopping. They returned all smiles and hopped up on sugar, Emilia lugging along a pink Barbie princess lunch box as well as a pink plaid backpack. The amount of pink was to be expected. The size of the backpack was not.

"Wow, Emilia. Your new backpack is really . . . big," I said.

"That's the one she wanted," Sandi said by way of apology.

The backpack was more than half the size of my five-year-old and appeared to be in danger of weighing her down when empty. I imagined that filling it with a mere pencil and sheet of paper would cause her to topple over entirely. She inherited my sense of grace and therefore doesn't require much assistance when it comes to falling down.

"I love my pack-pack," Emilia declared, and the matter was put to rest.

When the long-awaited first day of kindergarten arrived, she spent the morning in tears, fretting over the backpack, which she now realized was far too big for her tiny frame. We cast it aside in favor of one of the five thousand pink Barbie princess backpacks we already had. I put aside the pink plaid monstrosity, which will come in handy if we are ever homeless and need to fit all of our belongings into a single bag.

I drove Emilia to school on the first day and walked her to the playground. Being the tyrant that I am, I insisted that she wear her coat in the freezing temperature, even though it covered the pink dress she'd been hoping to show off. When the bell rang, Ms. Sherod emerged.

"Line up, kids," she commanded. The children dutifully did so. "Now say goodbye to Mom and Dad," she instructed, and then led them into her classroom, where the adults were not permitted. Mothers and fathers stood with expressions of abandonment, shocked that at that moment, our children didn't actually *need* us. When all of the children had made it inside, Ms. Sherod popped her head back out and said, "Believe me, it's better this way."

As I walked back to my car with a tingle in my throat, my heart felt light and fluttery. I attributed this not to the emotion of the experience, but to my heart condition that would surely cause me to drop dead on the spot. Then I remembered that I don't suffer from a heart condition so much as hypochondria, which meant that I wasn't going to drop dead, nor should I rush to the hospital to spend another two thousand dollars finding out that I still suffer from nothing worse than hypochondria.

I have no complaints with Emilia's school or teachers, except for one thing: They periodically lose my child or leave her unattended. Maybe I'm overparenting, but I prefer that the responsible adults not misplace my daughter. On one occasion, it was because Emilia was sad about not completing an assignment, so she hid underneath a table at the end of the day while the other children exited. At least she broke the rules because she wanted to do more work, not because she was trying to get out of it. There have been a handful of instances when students played on the playground in the morning with no supervision. Whoever was scheduled to be on duty simply wasn't there, hopefully due to sudden kidney failure or alien abduction, because there really is no other valid excuse. The unsupervised playground was disconcerting, especially when you spend as much time as I do fretting about all of the sickos and whack-jobs in the world.

One day I went to the school to retrieve Emilia, following her participation in an after-school program. I arrived seven minutes late. This is a parental sin, of course, but I'm only late for my children once every millennium, and this happened to be the day. I was rehearsing my apology and offer of monetary compensation to whichever adult was left waiting with her, when I pulled up to the school to see it deserted, except for my little girl waiting by herself, shivering and clutching the coat she refused to wear. She had a hopeful look on her face that could easily have turned to panic. I parked my car and walked to her. When she saw me, her eyes grew wide. She smiled big in joy and relief and ran to me.

"Mom!" she screamed. "I knew you'd come!"

"Of course." I hugged her. "I'll *always* come for you. But where's your teacher?"

"Um . . ." She looked around. "They left."

I hid from Emilia my disgust with myself for being late, along with my fury at the staff for leaving her alone. A volunteer had been assigned to wait with the children, and while I'm sure Emilia just slipped under the radar as opposed to being the target of willful neglect, there really are no excuses for such situations, not even aliens. Whenever I bring these matters to the attention of the school staff, they are incredibly apologetic and assure me that these mistakes won't happen again. Every single time.

In an effort to satisfy my curiosity regarding what goes on *inside* the classroom, I volunteered during the regular kindergarten portion of Emilia's day, as well as during the Chinese class. Volunteering never fails to renew my appreciation for teachers. Anyone who complains that teachers have it easy because they get their summers off needs to spend two hours (that's all it takes) volunteering in a kindergarten classroom. Suddenly you realize what teachers are up against. Personally, I would rather be a prison guard.

Volunteering in Mr. Li's class involved giving the children general guidance and keeping them in line. He'd just had a big talk with the class about how students are there to learn and not allowed to go to the bathroom every five minutes or keep getting up for a drink of water. Then a kid asked me if he could get a drink of water. Instinct always tells me to say yes when a child asks for water. I'd feel the same way if a child asked for a little more air to breathe. When my own children ask for water, I tell them they can have as much water as they want. As soon as I said yes, the boy shot up from his seat and ran to the water fountain. Mr. Li caught the movement out of the corner of his eye and stopped the boy, reminding him that only moments before he'd told them not to ask for any more drinks of water—each of them had already had a turn. The boy instantly turned and pointed to me with an outstretched arm and finger.

"Oh," I said sheepishly to the kindergarten teacher. "Yeah,

that's my fault. I told him he could get a drink."

Mr. Li looked at me, obviously contemplating the value of having me assist in his classroom, and for a moment I thought I might be sent home.

Nonetheless, I enjoyed volunteering in both the morning and afternoon classes. I learned to count in Chinese, and the environment is one where compulsive use of hand sanitizer is praised instead of viewed as indicative of a personality disorder.

Emilia adjusted well to kindergarten, just as Mike and I made the decision to uproot our family and move to Mexico for the winter. Emilia would have three months of Chinese, followed by three months in Mexico before returning to Chinese class. I anticipated that this would leave her either extremely confused or a linguistic genius.

We'd made enough trips to Todos Santos, Mexico, where Mike's parents live, to figure out how to stay inexpensively and continue to work from there. The difficulty is not necessarily in going to Mexico, but in extracting oneself from the States. It was time to have "the talk" with Emilia's teachers. Surely they'd judge me as irresponsible and naturally assume that I was putting my children in harm's way solely for the opportunity to get a tan and drink beer on the beach.

"Ms. Sherod?" I approached her at the end of the school day. "Yes?"

"So . . . Uh . . ." *Wow,* I thought. *I am an absolute pussy.* My heart raced. "We're planning on leaving for a few months to go live in Mexico. Three. We're leaving for three months, but I'll do *whatever* I have to do to make sure Emilia keeps up with the rest of the class. Is that okay?" I can't pinpoint exactly what I was afraid of. It had been such a process to get Emilia into the school;

maybe I feared that this trip could result in her being booted permanently. What if this resulted in Idaho school systems blackballing my children from their institutions and thereby forcing me to homeschool my children? I'd have to see if there were any juicy trials coming up. But Ms. Sherod smiled.

"If you have the opportunity to do something like that, you do it," she instructed. She leaned close and whispered in confidence, "It's just kindergarten." She was right. What a child learns from living in another country is far greater than any kindergarten curriculum. And Emilia would be enrolled in school while we were in Mexico. It wasn't as if she'd be watching television all day and eating tacos. But an even greater fear remained when I thought of telling Mr. Li. How on earth was I to keep up with the Chinese curriculum? I have many skills, but fluency in Mandarin Chinese is not one of them. Also, Mr. Li scared me just a little. This was not your typical smiles-and-rainbows kindergarten teacher. He was a no-nonsense taskmaster. Children didn't fool around in Mr. Li's class. Children didn't get a second drink of water. And no one wants to be reprimanded, but being reprimanded in Chinese sounds especially harsh. Actually, even being praised in Chinese sounds harsh. But I told Mr. Li, and he, too, saw the big picture. Both teachers presented me with a wealth of materials to take with us to Mexico and asked that I just do my best in terms of keeping up from afar.

Neither Emilia nor Ivy had any objections about going to Mexico, either.

"Do they have chocolate in Mexico?" Ivy asked.

"Yes," I promised.

"Do they have friends that are this tall?" Emilia placed her hand on top of her head.

"Yes, you'll go to school there, and there will be kids your age. And your height."

"Do they have lunch in Mexico?" she asked.

"Every day."

* * *

CHAPTER 3

The Burn Unit

"Mom, can we go *there* for lunch?" Emilia pointed to a strip mall, home of China Grand Buffet.

"No."

"But look, that's Chinese, just like at my school." She indicated the characters next to the words *China Grand Buffet*. Utilizing my degree in linguistics, I deduced that these characters meant: China Grand Buffet.

"I promise someday I will take you to a Chinese restaurant, but it won't be China Grand Buffet."

"Why not?"

"It's a family rule," I explained. "We don't eat at buffets."

Personally, I think buffets are disgusting and bear some responsibility in terms of what's wrong with this country. Whenever I find myself in a political conversation regarding Things That Are Wrong with This Country, I always offer up my opinion of buffets. I'm typically then shunned from further conversation, which reverts back to questions of church and state and gun rights and international policy and partisan politics. But think about it. Buffets are wrong on many levels. No one should actually *eat all they can eat*. This thinking is fundamentally wrong. An attempt to consume all that is physically possible for your body to consume is the epitome of gluttony. And the thinking that this is economical is severely flawed. The idea that you should overeat to get your money's worth makes no sense. It's not as if you can eat the next day's meals, thereby stocking up on your body's food requirements. The body can only take so much food at a time, and you're going to need to eat again later anyway, so stuffing yourself is just gross. I flatly forbid anyone in my immediate family from frequenting the buffets in our town, including any place with a name along the lines of Chuck-A-Rama. What does that even mean? Is Chuck the proprietor of this establishment, or does "Chuck" relate to "upchuck"? While healthier, more unique eating establishments have had to close their doors, Chuck-A-Rama is going strong, at least in Idaho. What's wrong with this country? Buffets.

Emilia accepted my refusal to go to China Grand Buffet, and when we arrived home, I decided to reward both girls with a healthier endeavor, but one that would still be considered a treat: I broke out the Slip 'n Slide. What I'd forgotten was that my children are too timid to enjoy use of the Slip 'n Slide unless they have older kids like their cousins to show them how it's done. It took me about forty-five minutes of wrestling with various hoses to set up the Slip 'n Slide, followed by another twenty minutes assessing and poorly remedying the leaks, so I was determined that they were going to have fun on the fucking wet piece of plastic, even if they broke their necks in the process.

"Just run and slide, run and slide," I coached them, but without someone to go before them, they refused.

"I don't want to," said Emilia.

"I'm scared," said Ivy.

"Come on, kids, this is super fun!" I cheered.

They held each other's hands in solidarity and took a defiant step back from the Slip 'n Slide.

"Fine," I said. "Wait here." I went inside and put on my bathing suit, which is a bikini I've had longer than my children. Deftly avoiding all mirrors in the house, I made my way back outside and demonstrated the run and slide technique. Maybe I've lost my inner child or forgotten what fun feels like, but I'm sad to report that using a Slip 'n Slide as an adult results in absolutely zero enjoyment. Especially when one is self-conscious about wearing a bikini that's three sizes too small. Bumping my way along the yellow plastic was an excellent way to highlight the jiggling of my belly. In addition, the Slip 'n Slide was in our front yard, and I wasn't enjoying the thought of any of the neighbors witnessing the aforementioned jiggling, followed by the pathetic lumbering of my body as I attempted to get up off the ground, cold, wet, chubby, and covered with unwanted souvenirs of nature.

Our backyard is enormous, the sort of backyard better suited to *Brady Bunch* families with oodles of kids, or people who like to keep dogs and chickens and goats, or someone who needs ample room with which to dispose of an occasional body. It is fenced on all sides and may very well have been used as the backdrop for a Slip 'n Slide commercial at some point in history. There is no reasonable explanation for why I would have set up the Slip 'n Slide in the *front* yard. Maybe I'd thought the neighbors would see my kids in the midst of gleeful summer fun and we'd instantly be endeared to them, at which point they'd decide to bake us cookies. But once I became a swimsuit-wearing participant, this plan backfired. We abandoned the Slip 'n Slide and went back inside. I forgot to avoid the mirrors this time.

Seeing myself in a bikini was distressing, especially in light of the fact that in just a few months we would travel to Mexico, where I would have frequent occasions to wear a bathing suit. I'd managed on a previous trip to avoid doing so, but avoiding wearing a bathing suit in Mexico is just as depressing as not looking good in a bathing suit, because the fact that you're not in one is a constant reminder of exactly *why* you are not in one. And even though I can get around it because I don't particularly like to swim or frolic in the surf, you can't drink as much beer at the beach as I do and eventually not have to visit the ocean for a quick pee.

I changed focus and tried on some of my old sundresses to see if they still fit. They did not, which I realized long before I got them on, because sadly, I could not get them on. I thought I might suffocate at one point when I managed to get a sundress over my head, and it began strangling my neck and arms, unable to progress any further down my body. I can't blame the sundresses, and I realized that they were at least ten years old. They literally had dust on them. If I haven't worn clothing in so long that it's gathered dust, chances are it's not going to fit. A decade is not kind to the body. A decade including two pregnancies is downright brutal. I momentarily deluded myself into thinking that I didn't *want* to wear the sundresses because after ten years, they were no doubt out of style. This is laughable, as nothing I wear is ever necessarily in style, and I faced facts that it had nothing to do with fashion and everything to do with the size of my body.

I told myself it was time to get serious, which I'd said on many prior occasions, but this time I really meant it. Sandi taught a Piyo class in town, so I thought I'd give it a try. I love yoga, and Piyo comes from the words *Pilates* and *yoga*; I thought it would be a good fit. The class took place in the upstairs room of a gymnastics studio. When I showed up, I noticed that I was by far the youngest person in the class. *I got this*, I told myself. But this wasn't the first time I'd given myself too much credit for being younger. Fifteen minutes into the class, I knew I was in trouble. Sure, there were some yoga poses, but they were performed at hyper speed. One segment of the class seemed entirely devoted to figuring out how to make pushups even more difficult than they already are. Is that really necessary? Pushups are plenty hard as it is. Even *girl* pushups are hard. Someone making you do pushups while keeping one leg off the ground or extended out to the side is both cruel and unusual, and I silently cursed my sister-in-law for being that someone. When the class got really tough, I looked at the unforgiving wall of mirrors before me and realized that while I might be younger than everyone else, I was also fatter. I made it through two classes (barely) before conveniently being busy during all future class times.

At the same time as my Piyo failures, I discovered Pinterest, the purpose of which seemed to be sharing recipes for disgustingly fattening foods, most of which fall into the meat-plus-cheese casserole category (the type that would nicely complement a Chuck-A-Rama buffet), and sharing various exercises, which one must undertake in earnest to reverse the effects of the aforementioned casseroles. I have one Pinterest friend who displays a frightening obsession with Marilyn Monroe. Thus, when I visit Pinterest, I am assaulted by a variety of half-naked Marilyn pictures, psycho-killer ab exercises, and directions on how to make deep-fried cheddar beer pork balls in lard gravy.

Luckily, we had an impending houseguest, one who had dietary restrictions that thwarted any aspirations I might have had of preparing the aforementioned pork balls. Kelly is one of Mike's college buddies and handy to have around, the sort of guy who can construct a working vehicle out of random items from your junk drawer. Of course, with all this knowledge and innate ability comes a ridiculous appreciation for things like *Star Wars* and discussions of electromagnetic fields and solar power and who would win in a battle between Godzilla and the Predator. These aren't things that I often think about or dwell on, so sometimes when Kelly speaks of these things, my eyes glaze over. He abruptly stops speaking and asks, "Amanda? Did I lose you again?" Sometimes a conversation with Kelly will involve how cool it is that a certain device has so much RAM or so many gigs or such and such bandwidth. I nod and smile with only a vague notion of what sort of device we're even talking about. Perhaps it slow cooks pork balls or harnesses nuclear energy. I stop him mid-sentence.

"I'm sorry, Kelly, but I just don't speak this language." Then he'll continue, trying to explain it to me in words I understand, dumbing down the concept so that someone on my non-techie level can comprehend. I interrupt him after another five minutes and say, "I'm sorry, Kelly. Now I kind of understand, but I still don't care."

* * *

Kelly's biggest struggle in life is with food, which is why his visit put the kibosh on pork balls; I just wouldn't do that to him. He's tried numerous combinations of diet and exercise, all to no avail until he discovered HCG. This is popular for weight loss, but also a chemical that the body produces during pregnancy, which goes against all logic, because the only weight loss associated with pregnancy is when you actually give birth or when you throw up from the nausea. And personally, I'm disinclined to try anything that I have to obtain from another country or that requires I give myself injections, which is how Kelly takes his HCG. Equally troubling is the idea that the body is supposed to survive on five hundred calories per day when using HCG.

"I need to find a really big apple," Kelly once said.

"Why?"

"Because today I'm allowed to have an apple."

"You're six feet tall, Kelly. Perhaps you should eat more than an apple."

"Don't worry," he said. "I'm also allowed one ounce of chicken with no seasoning."

Kelly talks a lot. In fact, Kelly talks constantly, so when he approached me in the kitchen one day but seemed at a loss for words, I knew something was up.

"So, Amanda, I . . . I was going to ask you . . . What would you think . . ."

"Spit it out, Kelly. What's up?"

"I don't know how to say this . . ."

"That's ridiculous, Kelly. You talk more than anyone else I know."

"I have some extra HCG if you want to try it."

The difficult thing for Kelly to voice wasn't that he was

trying to be my drug dealer; by offering me HCG, he was admitting that I *needed* HCG. In essence, he gave voice to the fact that I was chubby. As a male, he was well aware of how dangerous such an action could be. There is an unspoken rule that men must never admit that a woman is fat, despite the fact that the evidence might be literally overwhelming. If a woman sits on a chair only to have it break apart underneath her massive form, a man is supposed to help her to her feet and immediately begin criticizing the poor craftsmanship of what was once a perfectly fine chair. Women don't get fatter; our clothes get smaller. And one should never inquire about a due date until a woman explicitly says, "I am pregnant, and there is a baby growing inside me." We all know these rules. Kelly braced in the event that my head would spin around or in case I attempted to remove his heart from his chest with my bare hands. To his obvious relief, I responded with a mere, "No thanks."

During certain phases of Kelly's HCG diet, he's permitted to eat a specific kind of sugar-free pudding. This is the closest Kelly now allows himself to get to the sugar binges of his former life. The times when he's allowed pudding coincide with when he's also permitted to drink alcohol. When Kelly is drunk, he approaches pudding not with a spoon, but as a lover reunited with his greatest desire after a prolonged absence. He literally crushes the pudding cup against his face. The easiest way to tell if Kelly is suffering from a hangover is not from the typical clues of bloodshot eyes or a general air of queasiness, but whether or not he has a ring of dried chocolate pudding circling his mouth. There are times when I think we might need to consider a pudding intervention. As someone with enough addictions of my own, I don't need to add pudding into the mix, so this was yet another reason for me to pass on his offer of HCG.

Most women who struggle with their weight as I do hate to have their picture taken. It wouldn't be so bad if there was physically a means of sucking in one's neck, but as yet, I haven't figured out how to do this. I've heard women talk about how they wish they could Photoshop their face onto the body of someone thinner. I would take the opposite approach. I'd rather have my face Photoshopped onto the body of someone who is much larger. That way, when people saw me in the flesh, they'd think I look fantastic. Having a really flattering picture of yourself just prepares the world to be disappointed with the real you.

Though I worry about my weight, I try to avoid a lot of the other stupid worries that females have and the corresponding rituals that women put themselves through. Not all, though. Every other month, I have my hair colored. And every six weeks, I get my hoo-hoo waxed. I'd like to keep it at that. I don't need my nails painted or eyebrows threaded or lashes extended. I want to simplify, not add on. The human body requires a ridiculous amount of maintenance as it is. I see no need to add one more thing to my to-do list so that my eyelashes can look freakishly long. And as far as eyebrows, I don't know what threading them means, but I hear it's incredibly painful.

Waxing the nether regions is ridiculous and painful and expensive and unnecessary. I recognize this and once suggested to my husband that I should give it up, during a discussion of what luxuries we could forgo to get our finances in order. Mike responded with an immediate and emphatic *no*, both to the idea of giving up waxing as well as ceasing to pay someone to mow the lawn. Apparently he feels that landscaping of any kind, be it upon lawn or bush, is money well spent. So I'll continue to do it for him, even though it involves assuming the most vulnerable position one can possibly assume. Paying someone to painfully rip the hair off your asshole is about as stupid a thing as I can think of. And the fact that the client and aesthetician can carry on a mundane conversation about weather and celebrities and what to get the kids this year for Christmas while one person places hot wax on the other's vagina is ridiculous. This is the epitome of the stupid female ritual.

Another moronic thing women put themselves through is burning one's face off. I know it has a technical name like chemical peel, but really it's burning one's face off. I stopped in at my husband's office one day, where Sandi also works. She was wearing a huge hat pulled down low over her face. When she looked up, my first instinct was to call 9-1-1.

"Jesus, Sandi, what the hell happened to you?"

"One of my clients gave me a free chemical peel. I know it looks bad now, but when it all heals, my skin is going to look incredible!" She tried to smile then, but stopped when her face began to crack.

"Does that hurt?"

"Yes, this is unbelievably painful. But it was free."

"Well, I'm glad you didn't pay someone to do that to you."

The irony of making yourself hideous so that you can look pretty is startling, but we do it all the time.

At one point, we actually sent her home from the office because she looked too frightening to be on display to the general public.

"Sandi," Mike said, "I think you should go home."

"I can't. I'm meeting with clients."

"You don't understand. You *can't* meet clients."

"Is it really that bad?"

"Yes, children are scared of you. You look like a burn victim."

"Well, technically I *am* a burn victim."

"I'm going to have to call bullshit on that," I interjected. "If you willingly subject yourself to something like that, and you do so in the name of vanity, you don't get to put yourself in league with someone who was trapped in a burning house or had acid thrown in her face. You're not a victim; you're a willing participant."

"Did I mention it was free?"

* * *

Acknowledgments

There are many people who have helped me over the years and too many to properly thank on a single page. And my publisher won't spring for two pages. But I do have to say thank you to Mike Turner, Elizabeth Day, Ross Patty, and Tom Reale. This book would not exist in its current form without your support and hard work. It takes a village. No wait, that's all wrong. It takes a team of geographically diverse people with different roles, who may not know one another, one of whom may be my husband, to work on various aspects of a book so that the words all come together real smooth-like and without leading to any ridiculous, borderline incoherent run-ons. That's what it takes.

IF YOU ENJOYED THIS BOOK,
PLEASE CONSIDER POSTING A REVIEW ONLINE.

FOLLOW AK TURNER AND VAGABONDING WITH KIDS AT:

VagabondingWithKids.com
AKTurner.com
Facebook.com/VagabondingWithKids
Facebook.com/AKTurnerAuthor
Twitter.com/VagabondingKids
Pinterest.com/VagabondKids
Instagram.com/WhatWouldTurnersDo

ALSO BY AK TURNER

Vagabonding with Kids
Vagabonding with Kids: Australia
Vagabonding with Kids: Brazil
Vagabonding with Kid: Alaska
Vagabonding with Kids: Spain